A BARNSLEY LAD

To Volvo Press Office

best wishes

David [signature]

A BARNSLEY LAD

A Miscellany of Life

Don Booker MBE

Wharncliffe Books

Dedicated to
my family, friends, supporters
and everyone at the Barnsley Chronicle

First Published in 2000 by
Wharncliffe Books
an imprint of
Pen and Sword Books Limited,
47 Church Street, Barnsley,
South Yorkshire. S70 2AS

Copyright © Don Booker 2000

For up-to-date information on other titles produced under the
Wharncliffe imprint, please telephone or write to:

> **Wharncliffe Books**
> **FREEPOST**
> **47 Church Street**
> **Barnsley**
> **South Yorkshire S70 2BR**
> **Telephone (24 hours): 01226 - 734555**

ISBN: 1-871647-64-9

Printed in Great Britain by
Redwood Books, Trowbridge, Wiltshire

Contents

Foreword

R eading Don Booker's account of our early days in journalism it struck me we must have been mad. Most of the time we were cold and wet, the pay was lousy and there is nothing glamorous in recording the minutiae of life in a Yorkshire pit village.

And yet I wouldn't have changed a moment of it and I'm glad that the same feeling pervades Don's account of those days.

It proves the point that journalism is as much a vocation as being a nurse, a fireman or a public hangman.

I never imagined it would be anything like it was. I thought all journalists looked like Humphrey Bogart and spent their time with a telephone crooked under their chin saying things like: 'Hold the front page' or 'Get me the city desk'.

In fifty years as a journalist I have never used either phrase and the only time I found myself cradling the telephone and speaking to the office, I was saying something wimpish like 'Why hasn't the news editor signed my expenses?'

Our beginnings might have been parochial but Don Booker and I made one significant contribution to journalism; we invented the chinstrap for the Bogart trilby which was obligatory head wear for hard-boiled reporters of our generation. Don claims copyright in his book but I think I beat him to it.

I was bought a pearl grey trilby on my seventeenth birthday and wore it as I cycled around Cudworth, Royston, Grimethorpe, Ryhill and Havercroft in pursuit of beetle drive winners and pigeon racing results.

The only way I could keep it on my head was by purloining a yard of my Auntie Madge's knicker elastic and making a chinstrap. Thus I became the only journalist in Barnsley and district (and possibly the world) to wear a pearl grey, snap-brimmed trilby with an elastic anchor.

Don was so impressed with my invention he followed suit. Now that's not the way he tells it but my version is the first you will read and I advise you to treat his account with caution. As I remember it Mr Booker was a flat 'at man.

They were enjoyable days made more so by the company I kept. I have been lucky in that throughout my career I have worked with men and women who knew what they were doing.

My first teacher was Stan Bristow, a kind and caring mentor. My first working companion was Don Booker and although we were in fierce opposition we became friends and remained so.

I went on to do other things and so did Don. His contribution to journalism and the town he served is a significant one.

Local newspapers are important. Their function is to cherish the town and the people who live there.

In his time as editor of the *Barnsley Chronicle*, Don Booker wasn't universally loved. He wouldn't have been doing his job properly had he been the most popular man in Barnsley. But in the final analysis he was diligent in his pursuit of the truth and that's the best tribute to be paid any journalist.

He has set his story down and it adds up to a good and fulfilling life and I am glad and proud to have been part of it.

Michael Parkinson

Introduction

*I*t has been said that 'wouldn't life be simple if we did not have to deal with people'. I realised very early in my life that I could only achieve things with the people God had put around me. Alone, we are nothing in this world. People and places are fascinating, and my life's journey has allowed me to meet and live with the poorest and richest people in the world and visit Third World countries and those which can be classed as exotic. This has been made possible by my wide interests and fifty years as a journalist with the *Barnsley Chronicle*. Boredom has never been part of my life, and although local journalism does not reap big financial rewards, it is one of the most fascinating professions. A rich man is not necessarily a man with a lot of money, but a man who is really happy. At times my life has had much anxiety, but yet deep inside I have always been happy. The millionaires I have met have not been happy. They were still striving because they had not got all they wanted and therefore had failed to find success in life. There is a proverb which says: 'He who is happy is rich, but it does not follow that he who is rich is happy.' My travels to more than forty countries allowed me to meet simple people like Emma in Morocco who lived in a hole in the ground, had a stool, a tin can and three hens. She was religious, loved everyone, and everyone loved her. She was happy. Working for a local newspaper does not offer the privileges of world travel, but my continuing interest in motoring journalism did. New cars are launched throughout the world and to these events often in exotic locations, the world's Press are invited. When the Ford Cortina was revealed to the world, Ilkley was chosen and Grimethorpe Colliery Band provided background music. Meeting people, including the Queen on two occasions, has filled my life with interest, and the organisations with which I have been associated have made life richer. In the following chapters I am honest, frank and, at times critical, but I am a person who faces reality and sees life just as it is. I have been used and abused, but if you live a high-profile life, then it happens. It is often said we should live for every day. We should, in fact, live for every moment, and I feel I have not wasted any period of my life. On the following pages join me on the genuine journey of *A Barnsley Lad*.

Don Booker

Early Days

The 3 June 1931 was my mother's birthday and in the racing calendar, was Derby Day. It was also the day I was born at 12 Silver Street, Dodworth, a few miles from Barnsley town centre. I was baptised at Dodworth Parish Church on 5 July 1931.

Our home was the typical miner's two-up and two-down terraced house in a region known as Dodworth Bottom. The tin bath hung on a nail at the rear of the property and the privy midden - an outside earth toilet - was forty yards away. There were three sizes of hole on which to sit.

My mother Ada (née Pickering), had lived in the house all her life and my dad Harry, moved in when they married. They lived with my grandparents, Joseph and Martha Pickering, but we moved when I was three, to a new end-terraced house at 106 Barnsley Road, Old Mill. It was better for my dad who worked at Robert Barker's skinyard in Old Mill, and living at Dodworth had meant long daily journeys for him.

At number 106 there was an inside toilet and near the fire range a bath which had a lid, making it a handy spare bed. It was comparatively luxurious, because there was also hot and cold water on tap.

For those early years at Dodworth, I can remember only my grandma suffering from asthma and my grandad being a local personality, because in his younger days he was a top rugby player. Although a miner at Strafford Colliery, he had played rugby for Dodworth and Wakefield Trinity, being described as 'one of the finest forwards of the day'. He was known as 'Black Watch', because he could carry three men down the field on his back.

He worked in the pit for fifty years, along with my uncles Dan, Frank and Arthur, but the latter two moved from the village, Uncle Frank, to be a coal deliverer at Huddersfield, and Uncle Arthur, to work in the steel industry at Stocksbridge. After forty-four years in Silver Street, grandma and grandad moved to a new council bungalow in Gate

12 Silver Street, Dodworth, the house where I was born in 1931.

A tough-looking grandad Pickering (left) during his Wakefield Trinity playing days.

Crescent. Grandad Joseph was so pleased he walked out in the street one morning in his shirt sleeves, got pneumonia and died seven days after moving house. I remember him as a character full of fun, who enjoyed a good laugh and a few pints of beer.

There were two aunts, Hilda and Olive. They were a very close couple spending nearly all their leisure time together. At that period there were no holiday trips to the seaside, just outings to relatives and friends, while to go to Huddersfield or Stocksbridge, was a big treat. My mother had followed her father's sporting interests, and was a good sprinter, winning prizes at the welfare park sports day. Her most prized possession was a tin money-box won for sporting prowess, which I have today.

Aunts Hilda and Olive lived at Silkstone, and I became attached to the village at an early age due to spending many holidays with them. Uncle George, Hilda's husband, was an excellent joiner and lived at Brick Row where he had a workshop. During the Second World War he was a Sergeant in the Home Guard, and I remember being puzzled seeing him going to evening parades in full uniform with a rifle, but smoking his pipe. Aunt Olive and Uncle Leslie lived in the pretty Blacker Green Lane area near the famous dam, where in later years I swam, fished, rowed a boat and skated in winter. Owned by the Greenwood family of Dodworth, it was a peaceful place. Uncle Leslie was a keen tennis player and the groundsman to the Blacker Green Tennis Club, which used a big hen hut as a clubhouse.

Silkstone became my second home and it was while staying at Blacker Green that I became friendly with the McCauley family at Manor Farm. At milking time I would join them in the cowsheds where a traditional bowl of porridge was distributed. They taught me how to milk a cow and also to bottle milk in the dairy. How nicer milk tasted in those days, with a one-inch topping of cream in each bottle. Cholesterol was an unknown medical term.

The Army took over Noblethorpe Park and several regiments camped there. There was a sentry box at the gates to the park and the

As a three-year-old taken in J. Roberts' studio in Eldon Street, Barnsley.

Following dad's footsteps into the boxing ring.

soldiers would cross the road and wash and shave in the stream. Some brought their wives and these were billeted with local families.

I remember a wooden shop near the *Ring O' Bells* which sold sweets only on Sunday afternoons. At the other side was a fish and chip shop which provided a delicacy that by the time it had arrived at Blacker Green was set in fat.

Barnsley Road, later to become Burton Road, was a happy place to live. It was only two miles from the town yet surrounded by countryside – fields, woods and the nearby Aire and Calder canal with its horse-drawn barges.

All the families were friendly and held parties on my dad's allotment to mark special events. The terraced houses had allotments at the rear owned by 'Tight' Cawthrow, the rent was 2s 6d (twelve-and-a-half pence) a year. My dad spent all his spare time on his plot, breeding hens and

A 1939 schoolday photograph.

bantams. He was a specialist breeder of Old English Game bantams and had won prizes at the National Poultry Show at Olympia. He was also a renowned show judge. He was known locally as the 'hen doctor', because fanciers would call with their ailing birds and he would operate on them at the kitchen table, stitching them up with needle and thread. He tried everything to get my interest, but the nearest I got was cleaning out the hen huts and taking birds in wicker baskets to shows, or the railway station for transit to London.

While living at number 106 my first interest in cars developed. Ken Stephenson's dad had a Morris Minor with a super smell of leather, and neighbour Jack Hardy, a Standard, and later a Vauxhall. Those cars stimulated my interest in motoring. Of course they were all black and in winter were covered with Vaseline for protection. The batteries were removed for the winter and stored in the pantry until March. A pegged rug usually covered the radiator and bonnet and on frosty days, a paraffin lamp was hung in the engine compartment, in a vain attempt to stave off the cold.

Burton Road Primary School was only 200 yards from home. On my first day I met the headmaster Mr Griggs and my class teacher, Miss Hadwen.

Mr Griggs – I never knew his Christian name - had an office with an unusual aroma. In later years I realised it had been his Afrikander pipe tobacco. All teachers used pale blue tea cups, and I was fascinated how Mr Griggs held his cup, with an extended little finger.

Burton Road School fancy dress winners at a 1939 Christmas dance. I was Gordon Richards, the jockey on the back row. The miner in the coat-of-arms was Cawthorne's Barry Jackson.

Thinking it was the correct way to hold a cup, I tried to copy him but found it difficult. Again in later years I discovered the reason for the unusual grip was that he had broken the finger and it was never properly set.

Junior school years were marred by the Second World War and teachers being called up for military service. Snacks were also a problem. We took bread and butter sandwiches which were kept in the teacher's desk and on eating they always tasted of lead pencils. In winter the tiny bottles of school milk were warmed near the open fire. Oddly, the milk tasted of salt. There were few sweets available in wartime, so we ate carrots and turnips instead. Also during the war, school meals were introduced, and were excellent value at 4d per day.

Dad Harry and mother Ada on my wedding day. Also Derek Moxon, my best man.

There was no individual attention in the classroom and I could not get to grips with arithmetic, failing the 11-plus and thus going to Raley School, which happily was one of the few to have its own swimming pool. I started in the 'A' stream and after two years sat examinations for a teacher training class at Longcar Central School and a place at Barnsley Technical School. I passed both exams, and decided on the latter. Raley was an exciting school, not only teaching swimming, but also woodwork, metalwork and specialist art subjects. Also how to breed rabbits - in the school boiler house.

My dad had been a keen amateur boxer and attended the gymnasium with Charlie Glover, the father of Brian Glover. He had boxing sessions with me in the kitchen, after Father Christmas had delivered a pair of boxing gloves. At Raley School I tried my luck boxing the PE teacher, Mr Hudson, and finished with a bloody nose. Mr Henry Bird was headmaster and Mrs Amy Bambridge my form teacher. She was a music specialist, so my interest in the subject was helpful. She was a widow from the First World War, and at Remembrance Day services in the hall, she would play the piano with tears streaming down her face. One of her more unusual requests was occasionally to ask that we scratch her back with a school ruler!

It was while attending the technical college that we were asked to work at a harvest camp to help the war effort. Off I went with forty other lads to Whitley Bridge, where on arrival we had to fill our mattresses with straw at the local farm and slept in bell tents or prefabricated buildings.

The food was poor and the work very hard. We were sent pea picking, for which we received 2s 6d (twelve-and-a-half pence), for an eight-stone sack which could take half-a-day to fill. We put stones and lumps of soil in the sacks to make up the weight, but the farmer knew our tricks and emptied out our 'ballast', before weighing the sacks.

Beetroot picking was another trying task, and our hands were still stained red a month after we returned home. Food in the fields was sandwiches and Robinsons' Lemon and Barley drink which was made in enamel buckets. It tasted dreadful, and on the packet said it should not be mixed in enamel containers!

There were no school uniforms and we had a technical college badge stitched to our tweed jackets. A school satchel was rare and most lads had pre-war cases and bags. I knew of only one scholar who had a fountain pen - and his dad was a wrestler. There were three departments, building, engineering and commercial. The latter was on the top floor and because the students were mainly girls, we were told it was out-of-bounds. If you did not like school dinners one could go the the Civic restaurant in the Public Hall. Tuesdays and Fridays were special - peas and chips were on the menu.

School days were happy days, and in fact all my early life was happy, because I was part of two happy families. My grandad Tom and grandmother Elizabeth Booker, lived on Old Bridge Street where I spent, once again, many happy hours with Aunts Florrie, Agnes, Rene and Elsie, and Uncles Fred, Jim and Charles.

The following chapters reveal aspects of my adult life, especially my marriage in 1956 to Freda Clarkson, of Haigh, a florist and later, the birth in January 1958 of our only daughter Julie.

My dad retired early from his job at Samuel Fox, steelworks, Stocksbridge, and died suddenly on 11 July, 1973, aged 68. My mother had for many years worked with the Women's Royal Voluntary Service, assisting each week with hairdressing at local hospitals. She had become a member of St Paul's Parish Church, Monk Bretton. Shortly before she died on 20 October 1984, aged 76, she received from the Bishop of Pontefract, Richard Hare, the sacrament of confirmation in her home, along with Aunt Olive. A moving, simple service, at which I gave the Bible reading.

Our daughter Julie married local solicitor Simon Alliott, on 9 April 1988 and granddaughter Lucy Elizabeth was born on 11 September 1990.

Working Days

Jobs were difficult to find for school-leavers in 1945 when I left Barnsley Technical School, because all vacancies were first offered to men returning from the war.

I secured a place on a job scheme operated by Fields, the builders, of Stairfoot. We had to help tradesmen building the first council houses on the Kendray estate, and the tasks included knocking holes through the concrete floors for service pipes and wires. At that time, no-one had thought of laying in ducting before concrete was laid. Then I managed to get work as an apprentice plumber/electrician with Fletcher and Sharpe, who had a workshop and office in the cellar of Cass' clothing factory at the corner of Churchfield and St Mary's Place, opposite the old Police Station. The wage was £1 10s (£1.50) a week and my first day was St Leger Day at Doncaster, but I was busy repairing a burst pipe at a house in Brierley Road, Grimethorpe.

The work was made harder by the lack of transport. We occasionally had Jim Sharpe's Austin Seven Ruby saloon, otherwise we had to take everything by handcart, even to Wombwell or Darton. Sand, cement, piping and even Barnsley's first Bendix washing-machine to Dr Slack's home at Stairfoot. The handcart had to be pushed even in snow. Heavy steel central-heating pipes had to be carried on one's shoulder through town.

The plumbers had a knack of carrying a WC basin on the bus with their arm around the bend. I was mate to Alf Dunk and Charlie Wright, both back from the forces, but they did not like heights and would push me through skylight windows three storeys high to 'putty and paint' leaking windows.

Regular jobs were clearing duckets – outside toilets installed before the invention of the WC. There were hundreds near the town centre and they were cast iron pans that collected waste water from the household sink and at a certain level tipped the pan over and down to the main drain. We rewired the Yorkshire miners' offices in Huddersfield Road and the West Riding Police offices in Barnsley, often working in the cells.

There did not seem much future at Fletcher and Sharpe (the latter was a local magician in the evenings), so I started to look for a change. It was a pity really, for I had studied plumbing in the evenings at Barnsley College and came top of the S1 section.

The job situation did not improve. I had not only walked the streets of Barnsley, but surrounding villages looking for a better job. The number of vacancies were held in a card file accommodated in a shoe box at the junior employment department at the Town Hall where Jim Brannan was in charge and it was from here that out came a card for a junior photographer's post at the *Barnsley Chronicle.*

I went along to the Church Street office. The editor-manager, Ronald Yates, invited me to his office but the job had just been taken by my friend Geoff Richards. Instead, he offered me a job on the front advertising counter taking advertisements and operating the company telephone exchange at the same time. The wage was £1 10s once again, but I wanted work so I took the job. The advertising manager was a tall, smart, but fearsome Dickensian figure called Frank Jackson. He wore wire-rimmed spectacles in the 1899-style and was abrupt in his manner. However, his bark proved worse than his bite.

The editor seemed pompous for someone without socks and having patches on the seat of his trousers.

My first day was 12 December 1947. I arrived in my first dark suit, until then I always wore sports jackets, all bought by my mother and dad. I was shown how to take births, deaths, 'in memoriams' and other adverts and record every one in a book with a number. Business adverts were entered in a huge leather-bound ledger which rested on a high desk.

We had a cash box for the takings, but the money in the box rarely

matched the prices in the book. Frank Jackson got round this by cashing-up early at 4.00pm and balancing the book with adverts taken later. If he was 10s (50p) down, he would reduce the cost of later adverts by that amount, charge the customer full rate and the book then balanced. Cashier Roy Gill never discovered what he did. There was no need because at the end of the day everything balanced.

My duties also included taking the printers' proofs to the *Ritz, Alhambra, Empire, Princess, The Star* (in Britannia Street) and *Pavilion* cinemas, *Theatre Royal* (to Mr

Arthur Clay, later to become the Chronicle's *chief cashier, Alan Ridgill, who became sports editor of the* Daily Mirror *and myself on the paper's doorstep in the 1940s.*

Mitchell), Beesons for Mourning Wear, and of course the Barnsley British Co-operative Society. What a powerful business operation was the Co-op. Its members and directors rated its importance so great that it even put Barnsley before British in its title. In later years I became the company's freelance public relations officer and publicised its first supermarkets.

At that period there were few pages in the *Barnsley Chronicle*, and display adverts for medicines such as Aspro, Rhuaka Syrup, Beechams Powders and Bile Beans, were kept in a drawer to appear when space allowed. The only car firms advertising were Eyre Bros, Reynolds Bros, J.C. Snell and Harry N. Booker - no relation.

The telephone exchange was a red box on a shelf with flip-down extension numbers – there were only five – and a winder to make the extension bell ring. There was also a dictaphone inter-communication system which worked from dry batteries stored under the stairs. The system was a monster and crackled constantly when in use. Ronald Yates once asked to be connected to Qualter Halls, but the line was so bad I thought he said Halls, and connected him to the fishmonger. That was the first time I received the 'sack', in those days the *Chronicle* would dispense with the services of an employee every week. The next day, he gave me back my job.

The editor was a character, and one week he asked me to place an advert for him because he fancied playing golf. He wanted a set of

The first postwar scooter that helped to make both the paper and myself famous.

clubs, got a response from the advert, and on a Good Friday afternoon walked through the offices in plus-four trousers with a bag of golf clubs on his shoulder. He said: 'I'm going for a well-earned breath of fresh air.' The following week he placed an advert to sell the clubs – 'I've found I haven't the patience to play.' Then he bought a super Sunbeam cycle from Garners, Sheffield Road, because he wanted to get fit. He cycled to work from Honeywell Lane, but after two weeks placed another advert in the paper: 'For sale, new cycle, due to health reasons.'

In addition to office duties each morning I had to polish the editor's desk. On top of the dictaphone master unit on his desk stood the framed photograph of the company's first transport: a Morris Ten car converted into a shooting brake. I dropped the frame, smashing the glass and on this occasion was pleasantly surprised not to get the sack again.

The reporters' room was down the corridor and had a glass roof. In the corner sat the sports editor, Cyril Kilner – complete with cigarette holder – who every time he left the building proudly carried a huge portable radio suspended from a shoulder strap. It was one of the first postwar portables.

To work at the *Barnsley Chronicle* was as prestigious as working for the Barnsley Co-op. Soon I was writing paragraphs from St Paul's Church, Monk Bretton, for the Village News column and my first *Chronicle* piece appeared on 22 May 1948, concerning a youth club trip to Belle Vue, Manchester, organised by Frank Bletcher.

Each week I produced news paragraphs and even a boxing tournament report from the Monk Bretton Miners' Welfare. Editor Ronald Yates, said I was producing more copy than the reporters and invited me to join their staff. At first I refused, but then decided to take the chance. My first posting was to the Wombwell office with Tony Galvin. It was snowing so I called at the British Colonial Shop in Peel Square and bought a new pair of Wellingtons for 7s (35p). The journey to Wombwell on a Burrows bus appeared to take hours, but I was welcomed by Tony and he gave me a contacts' list to collect news paragraphs from churches, clubs, schools and organisation secretaries.

It was a great thrill to use a typewriter and produce copy for that week's Wombwell edition. We had lunch at a little cafe, or warm pork pies sat around an electric fire in the office.

After only two weeks I was transferred back to head office and asked to take over as the Royston edition reporter. That was a mammoth task for one with so little experience, for in those days the Royston edition stretched from Kexborough and Bretton in the West to Hemsworth in the East. The population was huge and the area had three urban district councils, plus six parish and rural councils, in addition to more than ten school managers and governors groups. I was expected to cover the area on a motor scooter which made me proud to work for the *Chronicle*. Sadly it was unreliable and at times I had to travel to the districts by bus or train.

Ronald Yates had introduced district editions of the paper, making the *Chronicle* one of the first weekly newspapers to adopt this idea. Circulation soon increased to 36,000 copies a week and at one time reached 42,350 copies.

One day I had a call to return to the advertising department because advertising manager Frank Jackson was ill. I did the job for three months, but was then allowed to return to reporting. Again, after a few weeks Frank Jackson was ill again and the assistant advertising manager made a request for me to return. This time the company chairman, Sir Joseph Hewitt, asked me to go back and I said I was tired of being swapped about. He told Ronald Yates I had been cheeky and I was sacked again and put on the dole of £1 a week. I was recalled after several months and given my old job back on the Royston edition where I worked for 20 years.

It was during this time that a certain Brian Glover, joined the department as a representative. A jovial character, Brian worked at the *Chronicle* during the day and at night was a wrestler at Butlin's Holiday Camp in Filey, under the name of Leon Arras, the Australian life-saver. He left to enter a teacher training college at Doncaster and subsequently became famous as an actor, especially in the film 'Kes'. He was also the voice behind the Tetley tea man TV commercial.

During this period the *Chronicle* was the first town centre business to employ a security man. He was called Arthur Marsh and he was a dwarf. His duties included selling stationery from the front office

Brian Glover (centre) with compositor Albert Clayton and manager Roy Gill checking a page. Roy did not use a ruler to measure, but a ball of string.

and checking visitors. One morning the editor made a request that everyone arriving after 9.00am should be sent to his office. The ever polite Arthur said he would do so. The first to be late was the burly Brian Glover, who, after hearing Arthur's request, replied: 'If I'm going, you're going too!' He carried Arthur by the scruff of the neck into the editor's office.

There were regular threats to the editor from people who did not want their court cases to be printed. Several objectors had made their way to his office issuing threats, so Ronald Yates set up his own security system, a packet of pepper and a pickaxe handle by the side of his desk. Also three bleeps on the advertising dictaphone meant Brian Glover had to dash to the office.

My weekly duties in Darton, Mapplewell and Staincross, Royston, Ryhill and Cudworth included calling at the homes of secretaries of churches, chapels, sports clubs, working men's clubs, local Labour parties and any other organisations that felt they had something to tell our readers. Over the years I built up a strong bond with these people who became valuable news contacts. I did not realise at the time, but it was grass roots journalism and these calls were often the basis of bigger stories.

There was one problem back at the office: the availability of typewriters. For ten reporters, there were only two machines so one had to wait, or buy your own machine. New machines were scarce and expensive, so I looked through the adverts and discovered an Underwood Seven Bank for sale in Sheffield Road for £2. I could not believe what I saw, for the 'seven bank' was made before the days when two letters were on the same key – there was a key for each letter. It was a huge machine, but having bought it, I managed with difficulty to get it home on the bus.

Those who did not have access to a machine had to write their copy with pen and ink, the ball point pen was still a thing of the future!

Copy was set on the revolutionary Linotype machine, whose operators thought they were the elite of the newspaper business. They were men to be feared, as I discovered. Their galleys (trays) of set type were proofed by compositors and were then taken to the reporters' room. It was always exciting to see the results of one's labours in the paper each Friday. There was great job satisfaction.

Nearly every week someone was sacked. Geoff Richards was a regular candidate for the dole, on one occasion being accused by the editor of locking him in the lavatory. He had entered the place but someone, for a joke, put on the outside bolt – it was on the outside to stop intruders getting through the glass roof into the office. The editor shouted and kicked the door and was heard by Geoff as he walked by. He unfastened the bolt only to be accused by the editor of locking him inside, so he was dismissed. He got his job back two days later.

Supposedly a keen sportsman, the editor was more a spectator than a participant, but on one occasion he put himself in the *Chronicle* team to play Thurgoland Cricket Club. It was a friendly game, and on the day of the match he came to work in his white cricket trousers, visiting all parts of the company in his 'whites'. When it came to the match, he decided to open the batting and, after having his bails removed with the first ball, turned to the rest of the team waiting in the pavilion with the comment: 'That ball would have got Len Hutton out'. Hutton was then a top Yorkshire and England cricketer. Ronald Yates promptly got in his car and drove away, leaving the team with ten men.

Each Christmas the reporters were invited to Wentworth Castle at Stainborough, then a ladies' teacher training college, to escort the students at their Christmas party. It was a wonderful event with a huge Christmas tree in the hall and lots of lights and candles. The editor was also invited to escort the principal, and usually hired full evening dress from the Co-op tailoring department in Market Street for the event. At midnight, hundreds of balloons were released from a tower into the hall and on one occasion Ronald Yates stood proudly below while his photographer Roy McVie took a shot from the top. As the balloons were released, the students rushed forward and in the tussle a fire extinguisher was knocked from the wall, its foam spraying the poor editor from head to foot. He looked like a snowman. In a raging temper he said all staff present should report to his office the following (Saturday) morning at 10.00am. We were accused of planning a trick to ruin his night, which was untrue. Four

A dignified Ronald Yates (centre) surrounded by staff, presents a photograph album to Alderman Edward McVie to mark his year as Mayor.

reporters and the photographer were duly sacked on the spot, but by 10.00am on Monday were back in the office. The hired suit was riddled with holes burnt by the foam and he had to find £20 for its replacement.

Most people in the company including managers, feared Ronald Yates. Some would be highly critical of him and dash to his office for an outburst, only to change their minds before pressing the button on his door which would illuminate green if you could enter or red if you could not. During directors' meetings it would show red all the time.

A keen motorist, his first company car was a 1938 Morris Eight in which the Chief Constable, Mr George Parfitt, would also travel to Barnsley FC away matches.

During a trip to Preston Mr Parfitt lit his pipe while sitting in the rear and set fire to the roof of the car. It still had no roof lining when it was replaced by an Austin Ten, a car in which Geoff Richards and I subsequently had a frightening experience. Ronald Yates, always looking for ideas to develop newspaper sales, told Geoff and me to meet him back at the office at 7.00pm to go on 'an object lesson in news gathering'. Our destination was Grimethorpe, and as we drove along Pontefract Road there were many squeaks to which Ronald said: 'It sounds like a canary in the back.' But worse was to come, because it started to rain, both inside and outside the car. We were wet through. Rust had destroyed the inner wheel guards and we were sprayed with water from the spinning wheels. Apprentice Tommy Taylor, asked to clean the car, stood on the running board which promptly collapsed. He tied it up with string and the editor never knew.

The first new vehicle purchased by the *Chronicle* was an Austin A40 pick-up because it was easier to buy a commercial vehicle than a car. The tax law at that time demanded that the company name should be on the sides. The editor had boards made which would cover the writing, when he went on his nightly trips to a Newmillerdam pub. To improve road holding, five bags of sand were stored behind the driver's cab. He then went from one extreme to the other, buying himself an Austin limousine similar to the ones used for funerals. It had a sliding glass partition and a voice tube to speak to the rear passengers.

Next came an Austin A30 with an eight-horse power engine. Each year, with a luggage rack on the roof, he took his mother and girlfriend for holidays in the Isle of Man or Devon, usually leaving on Fridays to miss the weekend traffic, eventually reverting to Thursday and Wednesday for the same reason. He then purchased a sporty Triumph GT two-seater which he found cramped for his body size, difficult to reach the pedals when he wore sandals because of his gout, and because the roof line was too low for his trilby hat. It was quickly sold.

Ronald Yates, did not like to be overtaken by other cars and on one occasion in Lancashire, when a younger driver and his girlfriend drove ahead, he pulled alongside him at traffic lights and offered verbal abuse. A few miles ahead he was pulled in by the police. The other driver had complained and taken his number. When double white lines were introduced and it became an offence to drive across them, Ronald was waved on by a truck driver near Blackpool. He went over the lines, was spotted by police and fined. Again not liking other cars speeding past, he was overtaken in Wakefield Road by the Mayor's car, so he gave chase and nearly ditched the civic motor.

My interest in cars seemed to strengthen my relationship with the editor and he would telephone at all ours with his problems. On one occasion it was 2.00am when a desperate Ronald Yates telephoned from Sheffield to say his car had been stolen. I gave advice but he said 'I'm really worried because there was a woman's nightie in the back.'

He started courting a sister at Beckett Hospital and in the Spring of 1960 announced he was to marry at Holy Rood Roman Catholic Church. No-one from the office was invited, but we made a collection for a present. On the Thursday afternoon before the Friday wedding he called me to his office to thank me for the collection, but asked that the money be returned to staff because the wedding had been cancelled. He had a letter placed on the notice board saying how sad he was.

Everyone in the company was shocked and felt sorry for the bride-to-be. They all felt Ronald Yates had changed his mind, but thirty years later when I was editor of the paper the true story was told (I refer to this in my chapter EDITOR'S CHAIR).

There was no official training programme and when I enrolled for shorthand classes at Barnsley Technical College, the editor refused to give me three hours off on a Monday afternoon to attend. Instead I had to pay 2s 6d (twelve-and-a-half pence) for an hour's private tuition in the evening.

As far as tuition was concerned, one had to depend on the help from Tony Galvin, Jim Dobdy, Bernard Bennett, John Edwards - later to become editor of the *Yorkshire Post* - and Nancy Woodcock, who became John's wife. I believe Nancy was the

Nancy Woodcock

paper's first woman reporter and I joined her at council meetings.

When two sub-editors decided to leave the company, I applied to move into this department which checked reporters' copy, planned pages, and edited the editions for Royston, Penistone, Wombwell and Hoyland. I was given the Royston, Penistone and Hoyland editions. The work was very stressful and the trays full of copy took many hours to re-write. I joined Ernest Dymock, who was chief sub-editor, and Benny Hill, who had realised his ambition to become sports editor. Ronald Yates had experimented with sports editors from outside Barnsley, such as Don Creedy, from Blackpool, but they did not have Benny's filing system of Barnsley FC and outstanding knowledge of local sport. At one time, the editor would help with sub-editing the paper, but this got down to only the front page, which he did by joining us on Wednesday afternoons, supposedly helping! The only other occasions he came into the subs' room was when it was thundering and lightning.

He feared such weather conditions, and felt the lightning would strike the roof steelwork over the print works, and his adjoining office. Outside his office was a yard where in a storm water would collect. Then he feared it would flood his office and again he would move upstairs. He had a garden made in the yard, but it was sheltered and nothing grew – so he had it painted green. Benny Hill liked to store sweets and chocolate in his top drawer and when he told the editor he thought there were some mouse droppings Ronald picked up the telephone and contacted the RSPCA with a request: 'Can you send a cat to the *Chronicle*.' There was no response.

Ernest Dymock, myself and Benny Hill sporting bow ties for the actress. We were the Super Subs!

He always delighted in welcomingVIPs to the paper, and when the *Empire* cinema had been refurbished after a fire, a film star of the day named Lana Morris, came to re-open the cinema. She visited the *Chronicle* and Ernest, Benny and myself decided to wear bow ties. He brought her party into the subs' room, introduced me, Ernest and then paused before introducing the junior sports writer as Selwyn Lloyd, who was Chancellor of the Exchequer at the time. He should have said Selwyn Dunford.

The editor loved to show off his purchases to the staff. On one occasion he bought a pair of binoculars. He looked through the subs' window with them and said: 'Donald, I can see the Post Office.' I thought, 'so he should', it was only in Regent Street, 200yd away.

The binoculars were also used to spot staff in crowds at football matches. On one occasion he questioned why one Colin James, had been seen at a midweek game. Colin had left the paper three months earlier to join the *Yorkshire Evening Post*.

Work in the subs' room was heavy with some weeks nearly twenty changes of pages for the various editions. We were helped by veteran journalist Billy Heald, a true gentleman of the Press, who had retired after working for the *Sheffield Telegraph*, *Sheffield Star*, and as a freelance. He knew everyone of importance in town, as well as all the streets. He got annoyed at reporters who failed to get their facts right. Billy retired from the *Chronicle*, went to live in South Africa, but later returned for yet another stint.

Making sure the correct names were under photographs was always important, especially in the May local elections. There were times when the wrong names had been put under the small half-single column pictures and when the candidates failed to be elected, they blamed the paper. To avoid mistakes, one eve of production I stayed in the works until near midnight checking they were correct. Off I went home to bed but at 2.00am I heard something hitting the bedroom window. Looking out there was a sub-editor in the works truck asking me to return to the office. So, wearing pyjamas, a raincoat and wellingtons, I returned with him, because RonaldYates had got worse for drink and had placed his elbows on the page I had checked, scattering nearly eighty photo blocks on the floor. It took an hour to put things right.

For years the most popular column in the paper was 'Owd Sam' Sez, described as the weekly musings of a veteran 'Tyke who thinks he's got it all weighed up'. It was written by an anonymous local businessman who enjoyed having a go at Co-op directors and local councillors. He would also comment on items in the previous week's paper and his remarks brought many letters of complaint, because he wrote what others thought. When he decided to stop writing the column, Ronald Yates took over. He became the only Lancastrian to write a Yorkshire dialect column.

The old press could take a week to prepare for the early Friday morning printing of the *Chronicle*. There were always mechanical problems and when the resident engineer went on holiday, a replacement would have to come from Crabtree, of Leeds, to print the paper. One Thursday evening as we checked the final pages, the press started up and then the whole building began to shudder. After a few minutes there was a crashing sound, followed by a silence. We went into the print works to find the press room full of dust and a silent press. The engineer had pushed his luck by pressing the button that made the press go faster so that he could finish early. The press could not handle the speed, the foundations collapsed and all the wheels and cogs were smashed. We had to find the editor Yates, whom we eventually contacted at a Wakefield pub. On his return he was met by worried staff to whom he said: 'Show me the precise spot.' Being editor-manager it was his problem and it was suggested that he contact the *Yorkshire Post* to help. He asked for the telephone number which I reeled off smartly – Leeds 32701. He gave me a withering look and asked how I knew the number. I had memorised it during my freelance days. For several weeks the *Rotherham Advertiser*, also printed the *Chronicle*.

Reporters were always leaving and at times staff was at a low level. Junior reporter Stephen Richards was walking down the street and met his mate Ian Harley, who worked at a Wombwell textile factory. Stephen asked him if he would like to be a reporter. Ian thought a bit, and said he would. Stephen took him back to see the editor and he appointed him immediately. It was February 1969 when Ronald Yates checked some Thursday pages, went home and died suddenly.

His dying wish was that his coffin be borne by staff, and Stan Hathaway, Jack Bradley, Don Bottomley, Granville Wilson, Stephen Richards and I were asked to carry out the duty. We agreed and carried it on ice covered paths to the Wesleyan Church, Penistone, then up the hillside to his grave in the council cemetery. It was treacherous, and we thought he had made us work right to the end. The strain of the coffin-bearing task left Stan and Granville with back problems for years. Earlier, the undertaker had called me because he had got the coffin stuck in the bungalow entrance. I had to stand it upright and manoeuvre it towards the door. One Easter Tuesday Stan's back pain became so severe he asked us to take him to hospital. We tried to get him into my Morris Minor, but he could not bend. He was crying out with pain so Jack and I went to Beckett Hospital and collected a patient's trolley which we wheeled to the *Chronicle* office and then trundled Stan along Eastgate and Church Street to the casualty department.

Tony Galvin was soon appointed editor and I was asked to replace him as chief reporter. I was not too keen on the idea because I enjoyed my freedom working in a district and meeting people. I also thought of the former chief Vivian Turner, a brilliant journalist who appeared to live on pork pies, walnuts and beer. He would crush walnuts with a lead paper weight. He wrote his copy in pencil and was eventually sacked for being drunk and singing the 'Red Flag' outside the public hall on local election night.

Eventually I took the job but working conditions were poor. John Bayne, who had worked for Beaverbrook Newspapers in the north, was appointed general manager in April 1969 and set about improving staff conditions. The reporters' room had been moved to the top floor where staff had worked – and slipped – on the hardboard floor for years. He provided fitted carpet, new desks and typewriters. As chief reporter, I had to organise the news room and there were few reporters available, yet one day Ian Harley came to tell me he was to attend Barnsley Technical College. I asked if it was to study shorthand, and his reply was: 'No, textile science.' I could not believe what I heard and after further questioning was told that Ronald Yates had advised him to continue studying for the job he had left, not the job he had taken at the *Chronicle*. The classes were promptly cancelled.

The remaining months of 1969 were hectic, because the family owned and independent *Chronicle* was replacing its giant printing press which had been in use at the Eastgate works since the company moved there from Peel Square in 1910.

A new press was on the horizon and it was to be a Linotype Newsmaster, the first of its type in the UK and Europe. It was a Web-offset press, a new printing concept that gave better picture reproduction and offered more pages. The *Chronicle* had previously been limited to a maximum of twenty-four pages which was proving insufficient. At the time the paper cost six pence and plans were made for better news and feature cover.

The big day was 30 January 1970, when the *Chronicle* said 'Good Morning' to its readers with a 32-page paper, still costing only 6d (2.5p).

The paper had special pages for women, young people, television viewers, book reviews, motoring, entertainment and a 'Bible Says...'

feature written by Jehovah's Witness, Roni Wilkinson. All denominations had been invited to write this feature but failed to respond, until they learned a Witness had accepted the task!

In the 1990s big photographs in newspapers took over from big stories. It was felt that while people like instant coffee and instant foods, they also wanted instant news similar to that provided by national tabloid papers such as the *Mirror*. The *Chronicle* provided half-page photographs in 1970 whenever space allowed.

During this period I learnt to beware of the Linotype operators, whose little area beneath the editor's office window, was once described by printer Tommy Taylor as the 'royal enclosure'. They never appeared happy unless they were working overtime, and it was alleged that on Wednesday's they would sit on copy until 5.30pm so they could work overtime. When it was decided to carry the Thursday local election results in the Friday paper, it meant they would have to work even later, but they were paid until midnight, even if they finished at 8.00pm. Harold Higson said all week that we would have to get our act together, with no mistakes, but, it was the Linotype operators who never planned what to do. When the first results went to the print works for setting, there was a silence. The machines would not work. They had forgotten to re-set the time switches on their machines and the hot lead pots were stone cold. There were red faces among the Linotype operators, but smiles from the editorial department. These operators appeared to rule production, rather than Works Manager, Charlie Plumpton.

The editor was friendly with the manager of the *Empire* cinema who scored points with his employers each time his cinema was mentioned in the *Chronicle*. He won awards for the mentions, and in return offered free seats to *Chronicle* staff. Some went in the afternoon and it often happened that the names of staff were flashed up on the screen, telling them to return to the office.

Sir Joseph Hewitt had started making more regular visits to the paper, and one day he called me into the office. I feared it was another sacking, but he said he had an apology to make. He said he was sorry I had been sacked in the past, and he now realised he should have sacked the editor instead. I thanked him for his kindness which came more than twenty years after the event.

The *Chronicle* went from strength to strength, but in September 1973, Sir Joseph Hewitt died at his home near Filey.

Eventually, Tony Galvin became managing editor and I was appointed editor, feeling privileged to head what I believe to be Yorkshire's finest weekly newspaper.

Musical Journey

Music formed a major part of my life from an early age, the age of three, in fact.

The Booker family were keen bandsmen, with the lead being taken by my grandfather Tom, who was secretary of and played the double B Flat with, the National Reserve Band, a military band, which was a rarity in brass band county. The difference being that military bands include reed instruments.

Uncle Jack played trumpet, Uncle Jim clarinet and Uncle Charles cymbals. There were four members of the family in the band, with Victor Mason as bandmaster.

My earliest recollections were of seeing them all leading parades through Barnsley, and my visits to the band room at the National Reserve Club in Harborough Hill Road. I was provided with a uniform that was several sizes too big, which had been stored in a fusty cupboard under the stairs, but I thought it was wonderful, especially the cap with a peak.

Later in life I was in contact with the band on Mayor's Sunday which I was covering as a reporter, on which occasion the band made the headlines when it headed the wrong way through the town centre and left the civic parade to march the correct route without music.

My dad never joined the band, but was keen for me to maintain an interest. At the age of five my Christmas surprise was a miniature drum kit which cost 12s (60p) by mail order from the *Daily Express*. Really, it wasn't a surprise to me because I had discovered the kit hidden under a cushion behind a settee long before Christmas.

It formed the basis of a long association with dance bands, and when I was eight I was bought a much bigger drum kit, this time costing £8, from Neal's music shop in Sheffield Road, Barnsley.

Although not full-size, it was a kit few lads owned. The drum had a skin on only one side so the rest of the items could be stored inside and the lot was carried in a huge suitcase.

It was then that my friend Trevor Slater, an accomplished pianist at the age of ten, joined with me to play at concerts at Burton Road Junior School which we attended. Later we were joined by other musicians including violinist Roy Leach and accordionist Gerald Roden, and we played at youth clubs and local dances because more senior musicians were serving with the Armed Forces.

We regularly played at the old Arcadian Hall, above the Co-op restaurant, for the Co-operative Society's youth club. It was here that we were assured of Christmas cake and pudding after our show. The little ballroom was also used as a store for the restaurant and they kept bags of currants and raisins behind the stage screens. We would fill our pockets for our parents, never revealing the source of such wartime treasures. The caretaker at the Arcadian was never noted for his pleasant disposition and would regularly start spreading sawdust and sweeping the floor during the last waltz so he could get home early.

During the same period we entered several local talent competitions and my most embarrassing moment came during a Friday night talent show at the *Ritz* cinema. We asked for an hour's pause in our Co-op dance programme so that we could dash to the cinema. During our competition piece my side drum rolled off its stand, rumbled along the stage and crashed down into the organ pit. On that occasion we were unplaced!

The drum kit was difficult to transport and I had to wait for double decker buses so that it could go under the stairs, or my dad and I would set off two hours before a dance and carry the outfit. To have a big drum with only one skin was embarrassing, so my mother made a black elasticated cover to fit around the rim. 'D. Booker' was painted in glue in the middle and then covered with silver sparklers. It even had a full stop.

After a year, Geoff Haigh who attended the same school as myself and St Paul's Church Sunday School, asked if I would join him in a musical adventure: the formation of a dance band.

We eventually played at many local youth clubs where dances were held on Saturdays, in addition to playing for the church club. We also had engagements at Barnsley Central School, known as the jam factory, for the old students' association. Our pay was 1s 6d (7.5p) which I brought home and put in an egg cup.

We formed 'Geoff Haigh and his Syncopators' band and were joined by Wright Mason (trumpet), Roy Clarke (accordion) and Roy Leach (violin). We were the only dance band in Britain still wearing short trousers.

Geoff was known as the 'piano wrecker', because he would remove a piano front to get a better sound. He became one of the town's best pianists.

My first taxi ride was with the band to Ardsley Club. Geoff began to find more jobs at working men's clubs in the area, but my mother and dad were not keen on one so young playing in clubs and that was when I left Geoff and the band. His brother Peter bought a set of drums and took my place.

Back to Trevor Slater and the little band, we were never short of a job for which we received a few shillings a night or played for nothing for miners' charities.

Jobs we regularly took were at Beckett and St Helen's Hospitals. Before Christmas we would play in the Outpatients' Department for nurses and staff and I was terrified. I had never liked even walking past a hospital, never mind go to a dance there. We had to walk past the plaster and casualty rooms which in those days had a heavy ether smell. Tonsil removal and appendicitis were common youngsters' ailments and fears of that era!

The nursing sisters would take us upstairs in the interval for a splendid buffet with something we never had at home, trifle. But I was so nervous, I just had to pretend to eat.

During the dances I could see patients arriving at casualty, and often blackened miners with broken limbs would be wheeled through on trolleys as we played quick-steps and fox-trots. 'Apple Blossom Time' appeared to numb their pain.

At St Helen's Hospital, we played at the New Year's Eve staff dance, attended by the then Mayor Sam Trueman. The ether smell was not as bad and at midnight, when the taxi failed to arrive, the matron consoled us with egg and chips. A luxury at the time.

The band broke up and Jay Rich, who lived in Rotherham Road, Monk Bretton, and had his own dance orchestra, but liked to MC events, asked me to play drums with the ten-piece band at Hemsworth Palais de Dance which, for an 11-year-old was like playing at Hammersmith Palais with Joe Loss.

The dances were packed with chaps serving with the Armed Forces, home on leave for Christmas. The dancers took me to their hearts, but I don't think some of the older bandsmen were keen on having a youngster in their ranks.

Victor Speight (not Sylvester), a fishmonger, came to my home and sought my services to play at old-time dances at St Barnabas' Hall and St Joseph's Hall in Kendray. I played for two years for Victor. It was handy at St Joseph's Hall, because I could take my side drum and other items in a suitcase and use the Boys' Brigade big drum at the church. The dances were every Saturday, and it was here that I had a music stand holding a copy of the *Green 'Un* sports paper rather than music. Dancers were so carried away with the Gay Gordons they never noticed when I missed a beat as I read the Barnsley FC match reports.

Keen to read music, I started taking lessons for the rage of that period, the piano accordion. I was quickly playing my first tune, 'Little Sir Echo', but the neighbours also had their daughter, Jean Hardy, playing the instrument and she had lessons at Bells Accordion Club. Imagine the noise when we practised daily in our front rooms. Music and dancing helped the war years along while village dances kept morale and spirits high. There was no television, just radio with Henry Hall and ITMA, cinema, *Theatre Royal* and dance halls.

Village halls and schoolrooms were the usual venue with anything from a three-piece to seven-piece band, members usually being drawn from players with the local brass bands. Those dances, some six nights a week, often included a whist drive.

The girls painted their legs with a tan coloured solution because they could not buy nylon stockings, make-up was also frequently home-made. Those were the days of the pink bra and suspender belt and with luck, black market stockings.

Transporting a drum kit was getting to be a problem, so following a family tradition I turned to brass and took trumpet lessons. Uncle Jack tried his best, but he made little progress with me and so my dad sent me to Jimmy North, who played cornet with the famous Grimethorpe Colliery Band. He taught me each Tuesday after school for 2s 6d (12.5p), and soon I had my own band at Raley School.

Christmas was great for we were invited to all the parties including the girls' school, where they entertained the band in their cottage. We had more Spam and trifle than anyone else in Barnsley.

At this time, St Paul's Church had its own concert party and we toured other local churches with it. It was at Silkstone Primitive Methodist Church where I made my trumpet solo debut playing 'Holy City'. It was a very warm summer evening, but for some reason a coke stove was burning in the centre of the hall. I was given a good reception for such a number was considered to be a classic. But after a few minutes I was overcome by the heat and instead of the breath going down the mouthpiece, it was coming down the side.

A quick decision had to be made, so I turned over two pages of music at a time instead of one and got to the end much quicker. I did say 'I am sorry ladies and gentlemen, but I can't continue.' My mother and aunt were in the audience and were disgusted, but the chairman at the end, said: 'Never mind young man, Winston Churchill once failed to finish his speech.' I thought that's all right, but he did a better job trying to win the war.

I passed an exam to transfer to Barnsley Junior Technical School which was housed in the majestic Mining and Technical College next to the Town Hall. It was like taking a place at Oxford or Cambridge.

My band at the Barnsley Technical College at the age of fourteen. Note 'Rythm' on the drum.

Again my musical talents were called upon as drummer and trumpet player and we had a small band which included Jack Hall as drummer. His drum skin could not accommodate the word 'Rhythm', hence it read, 'Rythm'.

In the school was Harry Swift, a fine young pianist who had joined up with Raymond Pashley (drums), Alan Ashworth (piano accordion) and Gordon Robinson (electric guitar). He invited me to join them at Racecommon Road Youth Club, and there followed four excellent years with the 'Rhythm Swingtette'. Gordon

Playing in Swift's backyard in St John's Road, Barnsley.

soon left the band for the bigger bands in town and I also think, because his dad thought my trumpet was drowning his guitar.

Considering the instruments, it was an excellent band playing anything from favourites of the day to our own arrangements of Glenn Miller numbers. Harry Swift made brilliant arrangements of big band numbers and on one occasion at Barnsley Baths, we played 'String of Pearls' for thirty minutes due to requests from Canadian soldiers stationed at Cawthorne.

The band was managed by Tom Pashley, a Barnsley Council stone mason, whose son Raymond was on drums. We were joined by Brian Swift (guitar) and thought we had got the world when Gerry Newton joined on saxophone and clarinet. Our regular spots were Racecommon Road Youth Club on Fridays where the leaders, Ma and Pa Brown, would serve national cocoa, potted meat sandwiches and *Quaker Oat* crunch in the interval. MC was Denis Gill.

On Saturdays we moved to Dodworth Mechanics' Institute, where Tommy Hirst was MC. That was a treat because Harry's dad was a butcher and he provided under the counter corned beef for interval sandwiches at this venue. Travel was always a problem with so much equipment, but now with only a trumpet, I could go on my bike with the instrument strapped to my back.

Sometimes we travelled in an ice cream van until the police followed us and told the driver it was illegal, and so we turned to an open-topped outcrop coal lorry with its very high sides. The police could not see us inside.

Our pay was 7s or 10s (50p) a dance, but some weeks if the attendance was poor we received no pay at all. We played at scores of dances for injured miners, even at Pinderfields Hospital, Wakefield on a stage covered in red blankets. We also played for prisoners of war. The band uniform was white shirts, red ties and grey flannels, good thick Yorkshire flannel from the Co-op. Then we went stylish and were measured for band jackets after we got a length of grey worsted flannel from an unknown source. They had red lapels, but were made by a tailoress who had only made coats for women. The result was jackets with built-up shoulders and shaped lapels. We looked like 'pansies' and the jackets were only worn once.

We took pride in our appearance and paid very high black market prices for Brylcreem for our hair. To be sure of that Tommy Lawton soccer-look, we also often mixed scent from Woolworth's with lard.

At the end of the war, we played at Victory dances, wearing red, white and blue sashes, again tape from the Co-op in Market Street and bought with precious clothing coupons.

At the 'Mechanics', the *Horse and Jockey* public house formed the backdrop behind the stage, and as we played we witnessed the 'turning out' fights outside the pub. They too, were a tradition after many dances.

The 'Rhythm Swingtette' was a great band. We loved every minute and got our inspiration from our visits to Blackpool and hearing Geraldo, Ted Heath, Billy Ternent and Eric Winstone at the Tower, Winter Gardens and Palace.

We were offered a Blackpool season - playing at the skating rink above Fairyland opposite the central pier. We turned it down.

Regular Bank Holiday engagements were at Towncroft Working Men's Club, Mapplewell, where we played to packed concert rooms throughout the night. We were also popular with fairground folk, and

The Rhythm Swingtette, with Harry Swift (piano), Gerry Newton (saxophone), self on trumpet, Raymond Pashley (drums), Brian Swift (guitar) and Alan Ashworth (accordion). It was taken at Racecommon Road Youth Club the night Barnsley and Newcastle centre-forward George Robledo presented soccer prizes.

played at all the Tuby fairground family wedding receptions at the King George Hotel, where the piano stayed on the floor and the rest of the band played on a huge table top.

Monk Bretton Miners' Welfare was another popular venue where it was customary in those days for the MC to sprinkle grated wax on the floor to make it smooth for dancing shoes. It was at the Welfare where a chap forgot the wax and sprinkled Oxydol soap powder instead - the dance had to be cancelled because everyone was sneezing.

While at the college I joined the Army Cadet Force, which met after lessons each Tuesday in the hall, or the Drill Hall in Eastgate which had a rifle range. I was soon spotted as a trumpet player and invited to join the ACF Band as a bugler. I agreed and became the smallest player in the band. The other lads had to lift me into the army lorry when we went to other towns and villages to lead parades.

By joining the band I was told I could wear harp badges on my sleeves and these could be bought from the Famous Army Stores at

The band without a name playing at Royston Secondary School, self, Eric Hewitt, Gordon Broadbent, Ron Harris and Harry Corns.
Below: *The Howard's Academy band in later years when we did a* 'This is Your Life' *on Stan Richards at* Keresforth Hall Hotel.

the bottom of back Regent Street. I bought two badges and proudly put them on my sleeves for the next parade. It was then the Sergeant Major said: 'Booker, whatever have you got on your sleeves?' I replied: 'It is the bandsman's badge.'

He replied: 'It is a b..... bandmaster's badge, you have got a crown on top.' So the smallest member of the band had appointed himself bandmaster!

My fledgling career in journalism meant working unsocial hours and so I had to leave the band. But then came a request from another group of lads who were playing at The Gym, in Dodworth Road, known in classical circles as Howard's Academy of Dancing. They were the Blue Lyrics, and played in a minstrel-type gallery. On one occasion they had an unusual band member – a chap who played a musical saw.

When I explained my problems associated with evening council and political meetings they told me not to worry and just attend when I could.

The 'academy' was very special in the Barnsley dancing scene and that is why a later chapter tells a fuller story.

My musical career was drawing to a close because I sometimes had to work five nights a week for the *Chronicle*, but local guitarist Ron Harris, of Smithies, would not let me drift away. Each Thursday he would call at my home in Burton Road to play Harry James and Glenn Miller records on our radiogram. Such an item was rare and it had been bought at the Co-op Radio Shop in New Street. It had a huge, fancy cabinet with very little inside and my dad converted it to an automatic player that could take eight records. He got the wires crossed and it played eight records all at once.

But Ron introduced me to Gordon Broadbent (drums), Eric Hewitt (sax and clarinet) and Harry Corns (piano). They had a band playing in the Wombwell area and we had a great time. For some reason the band did not have a name and we used Frank Hargreaves' music stands. At the age of twenty-three I called it a day, playing my last gig at Cortonwood Miners' Welfare when my last solo was 'Autumn Leaves', probably appropriate.

I never made the top as far as bands go but the musical years did help the war to pass quickly for a teenager. Being a member of a band gave me something to live for – and that was what it was all about in the sad years on the home front.

Football Tales

Sport has always been an important part of my life but there was little to enjoy in my childhood and early teenage years due to the Second World War.

Most young male teachers were serving with the Armed Forces, leaving ageing staff to run schools. At Burton Road Primary School there were few facilities for football and cricket coaching and then, if you weren't top class, you were left behind.

Gaffer Brien was our form teacher and to me he seemed seventy-five years old and weighed sixteen stone. His enthusiasm for sport was nil, and the Thursday afternoon sports period was often called off for a threat of rain. We did arithmetic instead.

Raley Secondary School had a football field, but again youthful teachers were missing. We played at break times on the field fronting the school when the star player was Tommy Taylor, later the Barnsley, Manchester United and England centre-forward, who was killed in the Munich air crash. At the age of twelve, Tommy, from Smithies, who had also been at my previous Burton Road School, had the look of a professional, but for his 'basin cut' hair-style no doubt created by his dad. Tommy was always modest about his brilliant dribbling skills and was one of the nicest lads anyone could meet.

At this time I often played football with my band mates, especially near Grove Street School next to Barnsley football ground. I had started following the Barnsley team from the age of seven and we collected photographs of our heroes from the Sheffield *Green 'Un,* for which we queued every Saturday night behind the Regent Street branch office.

The cuttings were pasted in a book and when we were on the field we copied our heroes. I was a left-winger, so I called myself after Johnny Kelly, the Barnsley and Scotland international. Gavin Smith was on the other wing.

Football boots were a luxury and required clothing coupons. I got a pair for 7s 6d from Stantons in Eldon Street and a pair of shin pads with thick cane stays, from the Co-op. We wore pre-war soccer shirts found in the church hall and all were several sizes too small.

We played in backyards, streets and any spare pieces of land. In King Edward Street, Monk Bretton, we played with a tennis ball between two gable ends, and it was during a half-time that I smoked

Cliffe Lane Rovers' second team - with nine players. **Back row:** *Derek Moxon, Frank Taylor, Beverley Jackson, Arnold Cooke, myself and Laurie Williams (trainer).* **Front row:** *One-armed Bill Driver, Gerry Thompson, Lawrence Swaby and Charlie Reynolds.*

A ten-man team, this time I was goalkeeper.

my first cigarette, a Craven A. The other lads were big smokers and would hide in the old Anderson air-raid shelters, which were partly uncovered, so everyone knew they were inside because the cigarette smoke was coming through the bolt holes.

My left football boot started to show signs of wear very quickly. The maker must have thought everyone kicked with the right foot, on which boot was a fine toe-cap. But the left cap went soft due to my left-wing operations.

My dad said he would replace the cap before the next day's game, and with his hobbing-foot, his back against the pantry door and near the open fire, he worked until 2.00am replacing the cap. The following morning, before leaving for work, he shouted to say he had completed the task. I was thrilled, but when I went into the kitchen, I got a shock. The right boot had the original toe cap, but the renewed left cap was square. Having no mould, it was the best he could do. It was a joke when I ran onto the field, the left boot looked horrendous, but the biggest problem was the fact that when the ball hit the left corner it went for a throw-in and when it caught the right corner it went off target. The cap was so big the ball never made contact with the centre.

The highlight of my soccer career came when a group of lads at St Paul's Church, Monk Bretton, decided to form a team to compete in the Barnsley Nelson League. We had trials in farmer Harry Cooke's field in Burton Road and farmer's son, William Chatterton, allowed us to use a shed in his backyard as headquarters. We met every Sunday night with William's dad, Eric, as chairman and local fish and chip shop owner, Mr Sommerton, was manager – the local Alex Ferguson of the day. Mr Sommerton was also famous for having a 'chippy' where the chips were weighed for each customer.

All the lads paid 1s a week to play, and Frank Chatterton was treasurer, keeping the subs in a treacle tin. The Sunday night meetings after church were around a coke stove and local dealer Denis Thackray would call in to sell crisps and minerals. Dressing-rooms were half-a-mile away from the field which farmer Chatterton had kindly loaned. Fred Pepper, a colliery fitter, made the goal posts. Only once did I make the Cliffe Lane Rovers' first team and that was in an opening game of the season with Cudworth Darfield Road Juniors. Other members of the second team were included because many players were on holiday. I remember Harry Reynolds, a weak-looking bus conductor, going out onto the field so early for a pre-match practice that he collapsed exhausted and had to be carried off before kick-off. We played with ten men and lost 7-0.

In addition to paying to play, we had to wash our own kit. Bev Jackson, a local taxi-man's son, was goalkeeper and took a liking to the smart roll-collar green jersey, so much so, that he wore it on nights out in Barnsley – until the treasurer saw him and gave him a warning that it had to be worn only for matches.

The first team had Maurice Mountford as trainer-coach. He was classed as the 'fastest milkman in the west', because he ran from house to house delivering milk for the Co-op. At night he had the team running around the village to get fit, and anyone caught having a glass of beer was omitted from the next team.

I was a regular in the second team, but we rarely had eleven men. At times we only had nine in the team, and the centre-half, Bill Driver, had only one arm. He had been injured in a pit accident, but knew how to keep his balance when jumping to head the ball. We lost more matches than we won but turning out for Cliffe Lane Rovers was like playing for Barnsley.

We had a trainer, 'Owd', Laurie Williams, who was like a team first-aid man. He had a bucket filled with cold water, a sponge, an old football bladder with the top cut off to carry water and the sponge to injured players. A smelling salts bottle and tin of wintergreen ointment completed his kit.

He limped and always wore a trilby hat, collar, tie and overcoat on the touchline. We usually recovered from injury before he reached us. I ended my playing days with Rovers, but my interest in Barnsley FC has always been maintained.

Most junior male reporters fancy writing sports copy, and I had a spell when I travelled with Barnsley Reserves and covered most of their games. I travelled on the team coach, had meals in hotels, or if the away game was near home, shared an Albert Hirst pork pie from Eddie Fleetwood's carrier-bag.

The wonders of behind-the-scene work in the West Stand were not revealed until years later when I became editor of the *Chronicle*.

When the team was failing on the field there was always a steady flow of readers' letters criticising players or management. Some were published and some were not because they were libellous, but even at the end of the century some of the correspondents still condemn me for not publishing their highly critical letters about the club.

When Alan Clarke was manager there was a period when he refused to speak to sports editor Keith Lodge because he did not agree with one of his match reports. Keith also edited the club programme and for one home match the manager's column was blank because he was still not speaking to him.

A dream came true in December 1993 when at last I was cheered onto the Oakwell pitch. Not to play, but to present a cheque to Brendan O'Connell, who then returned it for the Hospice Appeal.

Chairman Geoff Buckle invited me to meet 'Sniffer' in his office to sort things out. My welcome from the former Don Revie star was simple: 'You are privileged to be able to speak to me.' I certainly was.

The problem was sorted out, but it was the time when every business in Barnsley was suffering from the year-long miners' strike. When that season closed, some officials thought another ball would never be kicked at Oakwell. To raise money for players, the club launched the Oakwell Centenary Society at a dinner at Ardsley House Hotel intending to raise £88,000 a year, but fewer than ten members were attracted. Then the figure grew to 390, well short of the 750 break-even figure. I appreciated how important the club was to the town and advised the club directors to tell supporters the full facts.

They were offered the whole front page if they would provide the copy in twenty-four hours. They did and for the first time in the history of the paper, we offered sport as a front page lead story.

The response was terrific. Within a week the break-even figure was reached and within two weeks the maximum of 1,500 had been achieved, plus a waiting list of potential members. Gerry Whewall, commercial manager said at the time: 'The society got off to a slow start, but when the *Barnsley Chronicle* spelled out our plight, we were given a new life-line. We can't thank them enough.'

From his cramped cabin, Gerry worked wonders before the days of management structures.

The following week I appealed for free weekend car parks to attract more shoppers to the town. Within hours of publication, Barnsley FC responded by offering the club's two car parks free of charge to the community.

'It was our way of thanking the community for supporting us,' said Barry Taylor, the vice-chairman.

I was proud that the *Chronicle* had played such a major role in saving Barnsley Football Club, but no success is achieved without team work! When the *Chronicle* had seats in the new East stand at Oakwell, I invited, among other guests, the Bishop of Wakefield, Nigel McCulloch. When he arrived, one supporter remarked, 'Blimey, I didn't think we were so bad.' But the Bishop also got a surprise when he saw the team sheet - it included Bishop, Archdeacon and Moses.

Over the years *Chronicle* editors interested in football, were given complimentary ticket for matches. That happened to me, but when I retired, I joined the list of season ticket holders.

Football is the greatest game of all and we were all delighted when Barnsley gained promotion to the Premier League in the 1997-1998 season. After many seasons when the club had struggled with small 'gates' things quickly got better.

Everyone was backing Barnsley and followed every game. When I arrived in Dijon in France to test the new Jaguar XK8 for the *Chronicle* and a magazine in Tenerife their PR men, Joe Greenwell and Martin Broomer, were standing on the steps of the chateau with the full-time score. Sadly it was the time we lost 6-0 against Chelsea!

My 'It's like watching Brazil' shirt was worn at breakfast at the finest hotels in Europe when I was there to road test cars. People loved it, but a sad point about Barnsley's success was the number of folk who came out of the woodwork claiming to be life-long supporters of the club, posing for the cameras and saying how their dads had taken them to matches. The directors' box was always full then, but they were not there regularly when the team was in the lower divisions. We also suddenly got a poet-in-residence.

To go to Wembley in May 2000 was a dream come true. Barnsley at Wembley? The result did not matter, but it was just what the team and town deserved after traumatic years. People, I find, love Barnsley.

Life on Wheels

My interest in four-wheeled transport stems from the encouragement given as a lad, by my Uncle Jack. Each summer he would say: 'Get thissen four wheels an'l make thi a trolley.' Off I would go around Old Bridge Street, Barnsley, to find a family with a pram that was near the end of its service. They were usually parked under the front window of the houses.

I would knock and ask the woman if she wanted to sell her pram. Times were hard in the 1930s and more often than not I would come away with a pram after paying 2s 6d (12.5p).

If I could manage to secure a high coach-built pram with two large wheels and two small ones I knew from experience that the trolley would have improved steering and roadholding.

For years I always looked forward to the summer, not for a day trip to Blackpool, but for a trolley.

'Mi Uncle Jack' was an expert, self-taught joiner, whose skill was under estimated by his employers. He had a hard task, repairing wooden coal wagons in the open and in all weathers. At home he had a stable-like workshop in the backyard. In the corner of which, standing on bricks, was a smart cabinet in which were stored his tools.

I would strip down the pram and hand the axles and wheels to my uncle who would build the trolley from spare wood. A steel bolt held together the front steering board and the main body of the trolley. We found that the steel ceiling roses that held those fancy light bowls which hung on chains, made ideal steering linkages.

If wood was short I would go to Eldon Street North Co-op and buy a Gamages soap-box for 6d which gave the trolley an instant body with appalling aerodynamics.

To me, a trolley and the mobility were exciting because I had never had a pedal car or three-wheeled bike.

I spent hours with 'mi Uncle Jack' in that shed. He smoked Woodbines and threw his tabs on the brick floor. When he turned away I picked them up and dashed down the yard to the closet where I finished them off.

It appeared I was on a good thing until one day my dad asked: 'What's this I hear about you smoking lad?' I was shocked and said I did not know what he was talking about.

'Yer Uncle Jack sez he's seen ya picking em up off floor,' he replied. He said 'Stop it' and I have not smoked since. From the corner of his eye 'mi Uncle Jack' had seen me up to my tricks.

At that time most youngsters dreaded the 11-plus examination. Most were promised a new bike if they passed the examination – what a dream. But I had no chance. Three years later the offer was made to me if I could pass the entrance examination to Barnsley Junior Technical School. At the same time I sat a special examination for a teachers' course at Longcar Central School. I passed them both, clearly my spell at Raley School was not completely wasted!

Before that I had attended Burton Road School where I think I spent more time cleaning out the fish pond than attending lessons.

The promise of the new bike had been made, but never materialised because in my dad's trade as a fellmonger, things were bad in summer and he was on short-time working. Fellmongers graded wool from sheep's pelts, and Barkers, where my dad worked, had a skinyard in Old Mill.

For weeks I had looked in Caffrey's shop in Doncaster Road and Garner's in Sheffield Road, not at gleaming bikes, there was no chrome or bright fittings in wartime, but at matt black bikes.

No, I did not get that new bike! I was back in the workshop with 'mi Uncle Jack' who said I could have his bike which had been re-built, but was rusty after hanging for three years on rope from the roof beams.

The bike with no name was re-built, but spares were short. I used sticky tape to repair punctures and often had three a day because the inner tubes would nip against the wheel rim. That bike was upside down resting on its handlebars and seat more often than it was on its wheels!

Eventually, when things got better, I rebuilt the bike with a three speed hub in the rear, a Lucas dynamo system and chrome semi-sporting handlebars. It was kept in the coal house, but one morning I discovered it had been stolen. It was never seen again.

To this day I still think about the bike I would have loved the Elswick with semi drop handlebars. They say what you have not had you never miss, but I miss the thrills I am sure that bike would have provided.

As far as four-wheeled transport was concerned there was little about during the war years, but my dad and a neighbour shared a big Austin for two days a week to operate an egg round and I often travelled with them.

I was fortunate, too, that the Hardy family next door had a

Standard Ten 1930s model with wire wheels. It was well cared for and Jack Hardy would often borrow my cycle tools to repair his car. In return he would take me on trips to the moors or when petrol allowed, for a rare visit to Scarborough. Later he then bought a Vauxhall and eventually he taught me to drive a car.

Always excited by anything on wheels, my driving test was passed on a Swallow Gadabout, the first motor scooter to be made after the war, by the same company that made Jaguar cars and Swallow sidecars. It was provided by the *Barnsley Chronicle* for my large news round, but had many problems. The engine was a 125cc Villiers and was under the seat with no means of ventilation. I had to stop after every four miles, lift the seat, and allow things to cool down. It became such a problem that I got a tin opener and cut two vents each side of the panel to make an air flow – matters improved.

My scooter became well-known in the area because on the side it read '*Barnsley Chronicle – Workers' Weekly*'. Provided by George Ward in Doncaster Road, it cost a fortune in maintenance but I loved it and found it exciting. Reporter Tony Galvin was also given a similar scooter to cover his rounds, but never passed his driving test and finished with the machine when it slid under a double-decker bus outside Albert Hirst's pork shop.

I asked for that scooter to rebuild in my dad's greenhouse. I spent months preparing the engine and cable work until it was 100 per cent. It was then that I asked Sir Joseph Hewitt, the *Chronicle* chairman, if I could buy the wrecked 'gadabout', but he refused and took it to Scarborough – where he lived – and sold it to a dealer.

My first motor cycle was a BSA C11 250cc with girder forks. It cost £60 and was the machine Michael Parkinson and I used for two years on our news rounds. Then followed a BSA 250 with telescopic forks, a Triumph 350 Twin and a further seven bikes, ending with a BSA Bantam from Garners in Pontefract Road, Barnsley, the main dealers.

Motorcycles had formed a major part of my life, mainly because they provided the cheapest form of transport. Then I spotted an advertisement in the *Chronicle*. It read:

Flying Officer would like to sell his Standard Flying Eight because of overseas duty. Price £234, Doncaster Road, Darfield.

My transport arrangements progressing from two wheels to four was about to take place. The BSA Bantam was sold for £100 and that was my passport to four wheels.

Left behind were my wellingtons, flat cap, and old overcoat – there

My first car, a 1946 Standard Flying Eight.

were no all-weather motor cycle outfits in those days – and at last I could collect news wearing my best suit and smart brown trilby hat which had that American film star look because there was braid around the brim.

Flying Officer Newman had convinced me that his 1946 Standard was a good runner – they used that term in those days. After reading what motoring writers advised – and still do – about getting a second opinion, I did just that.

My mate Geoff Bland was a mechanic so I paid him £5 to look the car over. His findings were that it required some body repairs, but was mechanically sound.

How right he was. In the next twelve months I spent £125 on repairs to the Flying Eight, a two-door model with a built-in weakness. The rear windows would wind down, but this meant there was no weather seal. The car's designer had thought about that requirement. He had included a trough under the window glass to catch the water and this was released through a tube under the wing. Things went well until the hole in the trough got blocked and allowed the water to spread over the internal wheel arch causing rot to the bodywork and interior trim. There was a rotten smell about the rear end of the Flying Eight!

Michael Parkinson and I were still mates and he had already passed his driving test in his dad's black Ford Prefect. Kind as he was, he would take the Darfield Road, Cudworth, bus to Barnsley and alight in Burton Road. Calling at my home where, with my 'L' plates fixed to the Standard, he would accompany me on the news rounds. For Mike it was also better than riding a bike or on the back of a motor cycle.

The Standard developed problems nearly every week and the apprentice at Geoff's garage used his wire brush on the underside of the petrol tank with such force that he went through the tank and it had to be replaced. Fine I thought. The muck will have gone from the tank.

Not so, I had an engine that spluttered and stopped. The new tank's packing had got inside and blocked the mechanical petrol pump. It was snowing at the time and I thought I would have to leave the car. But in those pioneer days of the 1950s one had to improvise rather than pay out money, so I asked Geoff to sit on the mudguard with a milk bottle filled with petrol. I removed the air filter from the carburettor and when I turned the ignition key I shouted to him to pour the petrol down the carburettor, it worked for a mile and I got home safely.

The car was fitted with Bendix brakes which, when set up correctly, were superb, but they rarely worked when the car was reversing.

My garage was made from old air-raid shelter galvanised sheets and was at the top of a hill. No-one left a car in the open in those days!

Taking the car each day from the garage was a dangerous operation. The fear of God struck into one's heart when those brakes

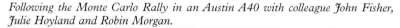

Following the Monte Carlo Rally in an Austin A40 with colleague John Fisher, Julie Hoyland and Robin Morgan.

The first Ford Capri to join my collection was like owning a Ferrari.

failed to bite. But I always managed to stop the car a few yards short of the main road.

I cannot say that I ever fell in love with that car although the smell of leather inside gave it a bit of class.

My old Scoutmaster Jim Winterbottom was keen to buy the car – his first – but he could not drive. He promised to pay me £250 for the 'Eight' if I would take him each Friday to deliver his brushes. He was a door-to-door salesman for Bettabrushes.

This I agreed to do, but it took him seven months to pass his test. All the time my sights were set on a Morris Minor Convertible owned by a BBC chap. At the same time I spent many hot Friday afternoons in the car that still smelt of rot.

Around me was every kind of brush you could think of – lavatory, sweeping and tooth!

In the end, it was off my hands. But Scoutmaster Jim then complained that the radiator leaked. I bought him a packet of Wonderseal, but it still leaked.

He was a very proud ex-RAF type who remembered his days in the desert with leaking radiators. 'We cracked an egg and put it in the radiator,' he said. 'It boiled and the air sucked the egg to the leaking spot, forming a seal.'

Jim did that too many times rather than get the radiator repaired. One day, negotiating Eldon Street North, the radiator burst and he had boiled eggs all over the screen. That blocked his view, and he came to a sudden stop.

I never loved it, Jim never loved it and it went out of this world without anyone caring. What a sad end for HWE 474, a car that carried the Union Jack on its bonnet.

During my news gathering in Royston I got to know the Smith family in Midland Road, where they operated the Royston Radio Relay Service. It was the period long before television when people rented a radio set or if they had no electricity laid on, also rented an accumulator.

The Smiths had an ex-American Army Jeep they wanted to sell for £5 and I asked Geoff Bland if he was interested. He was, and we put £2 10s (£2.50) each into the deal and he towed me back to Monk Bretton behind his old Bedford van. It was a frightening journey because the tow rope jerked and it needed all my strength to keep it on the road.

Once back in the workshop, we fitted a second hand exhaust system and went on trials down Lamb Lane and Burton Bank, this was before the big housing estates were built there. It caught the eye of local farmer and contractor Denis Thackray for four-wheel drives in those days were rare. He bought it for £15. We were pleased with £10 profit, but three days later he gave us another £10 to take it back because he was not happy with the vehicle. It was then sold to a Jeep enthusiast for £10. Possibly the best deals we ever made.

The Standard was followed by a Morris Minor Convertible bought from Bob Mozley, who worked for the *Sheffield Telegraph*. It cost £323, because that was every pound I could afford. I had it coach painted by hand by Bert Bickerstaffe of Cudworth, and had a maroon top with full view rear window made by the London Hood Company. It was one of the first wrap around rear windows in the country. Another Morris Minor followed and then my first new car was an Austin A40 from Eyre Bros., red with a black roof and costing £465. There was a waiting list for the car, which I eventually kept for nearly two years, but it had

In 1960 I was allowed to drive this vintage Wolseley car from Wakefield to Barnsley to mark the Automobile Club's 1900 1,000 mile trial around Britain. Also in the car is motoring pioneer St John Nixon (centre) and mechanic Arthur Ayscough.

The Mulhouse Museum at Alsace, has the world's largest collection of cars, made possible by the obsession of Hans and Fritz Schlumpf. Here I stand alongside the priceless Bugatti Royale limousine. Look at the length of the bonnet!

No, it is not Bosnia or a battlefront, but myself seriously considering if I dare get into the giant Chieftan battle tank. It is amazing what a carton of tea can do in torrential rain.

Here I set out on the award-winning journey, smashing a car on the way, and finding the suspension just as hard as that on a Morgan car.

to be sold to raise money for the legal fees for a new bungalow in Wordsworth Road, Monk Bretton. Because of low wages I was afraid to increase the mortgage to cover the fees.

It was replaced by a second-hand Minor sold by Jack Schofield at Eyres, and then followed a Morris Mini, VHE 11, bought from Smart and Batty, Upper Sheffield Road. The Ford Popular caught my eye, but it only had a three-speed gearbox. In later years, having a liking for style, I turned to the Ford Capri, of which I eventually had four. The car I always wanted was a Sunbeam Rapier. David Price, the Home Office pathologist, used such a car when covering local inquests. The price, at just under £1,000, was too high so for years I turned to Austin, Singer and Ford, before going back to a second-hand Morris Minor sold to me by Ted Johnson, when he was a salesman at a Conisbrough dealers.

In later years, when he became a leading Honda dealer in Barnsley, we built up a long association which continues to this day.

As the twentieth century came to a close I had a very rare motoring experience, I drove a tank !

During a Renault launch near Winchester the test route included a break with a difference, cartons of tea and the chance to drive various tanks. The stop was at Highlands Park tank driving course, where I donned Army camouflage gear and, due to the heavy rain, also had to wear a heavy rubber cape which made access to the tank's cockpit difficult.

Battling against the tricky terrain, I managed to handle a Chieftain battle tank with its rudder steering system. Consumption-wise, the tank covered three miles on a gallon of fuel, which was much worse than the Abbot self-propelled gun and the armoured personnel carrier which I also drove.

Later in the day I received a gold-plated tank from Tim Mack, Renault's director of communications, for being the best tank driver. He praised my driving skills and bravery in appalling weather conditions.

I feel my success was due to having driven Morgans for more than 30 years with their fly-off handbrakes. The experience made tank driving with huge button-release tillers much easier.

My journey to the end of the millennium was completed on 21 December 1999, when Ford invited me to their Journey Zone, and sections of the Millennium Dome in London.

Gentleman Jim

*F*ighting Paddy was the name by which thousands of people knew James Brown of Ryhill, near Barnsley. That is no surprise, for this Irishman, who was baptised a Roman Catholic, was brought up a Protestant and then served for more than fifty years with Royston Corps of the Salvation Army, was one of the roughest and toughest men to reach our shores.

During his life he had five names. He was baptised James Brown and was named James Brownley McClurg by his foster parents. At different periods of his boxing career he had been called James McClure, James McHarg and Paddy McIlroy. The name he kept for the longest period, however, was the one given to him by his real mother whom he did not meet until he was forty-two years old.

During my news rounds in Royston and Mapplewell in 1958 I met James one winter's Saturday in Towncroft Club where he told me his sad story. But like all good

Jim Brown on the day we first met.

fairy tales, it eventually had a happy and amazing ending. Throughout this chapter, he is referred to as Paddy.

Paddy was born at the tiny maternity home in Newry, County Down, Northern Ireland, which nestled in the shadows of the famous Mountains of Mourne. His mother could not afford to care for him, so at a very early age he was handed to foster parents. As he grew older he turned out to be one of the roughs of the village and delighted in causing disturbances at religious meetings and throwing bricks through church windows. In fact, he was biased against all the principles of Christianity.

At thirteen he left school and worked with his foster father, water divining and sinking wells at homesteads, for there was little or no piped water supply in the area. His spare time was occupied playing football for Silent Valley and by fighting! By this time, he was becoming keen on boxing and, knowing this, the local people put him into the ring to get a beating up and some experience. But he surprised them and not only won his fight, but won two more the same evening by the knock-out route, a feat which brought him a small silver cup which over the years was one of his proudest possessions. He would fight anywhere and was constantly challenging people to test him in the fields or barns near his home. After the battle he would invite his opponents home for a meal. His heart was really in the fight game and these open fights, where the hedgerows formed the ringsides, were really the start of 'Fighting Paddy'. He went on to fight thirty amateur contests and win twenty by knock-outs. He then turned professional and fought in the Chapelfields arena and in Ulster at the same time that Jack Doyle was making a name for himself. At this period, however, affairs in Ireland were depressed and for Paddy there were no fights and no work.

He spent much of his time poaching for game and salmon and also caught foxes and their cubs alive, for export to England. For the foxes he received £1 each and for the cubs 5s (25p) each. All the time his thoughts were upon the Lonsdale Belt, and longed for visits to New York, the aims of all great fighters. In fact he was so keen that he formed his own boxing club in the local blacksmith's shop, where he trained for long periods and at the end of each session was covered in the soot which fell from the ceiling every time he hit the punch-bag. Among his sparring partners was the eventual middleweight champion of Ulster, George Laverick.

He managed to get over twenty professional fights before he was twenty-one and his final fight in Ireland was under an American promoter in the Ulster Hall, Belfast. For this fight he took on a new name – Jimmy McHarg. To progress still further, he knew he must get over to England and decided to run away from home. Before he could leave the country he had to get a labour card, which necessitated the presentation of his birth certificate. This he could not do. After making some excuse to his foster mother for wanting the certificate, it was produced. The name read: 'James Brown'. This 'Paddy' could not understand, but she told him that a mistake had been made and it should have read James Brownley McClurg, the name which she had given him. For the first time in his life his suspicions were aroused and at the back of his mind he knew somehow that the people who had cared for him were not his parents. This spurred on his urge to get away and off he went with 10s (50p) in his pocket and a cycle which had cost £7 a few weeks earlier. At Larne, where he was to catch a boat to Scotland, he tried to sell the cycle to a local dealer who became suspicious, thinking the machine had been stolen, and called the police. After a time the police were satisfied that Paddy was the rightful owner and he finished by taking the cycle to the police station and selling it to a constable for £2.

The next day he arrived at Stranraer with £1 10s (£1.50) and a keen desire to become a boxing champion. Like so many young men, however, he was disappointed and the golden road quickly lost its glitter.

After a few days in Scotland he was down and out and had to live in the tramp lodging houses. There was no work and he made sure of his 'bed and breakfast' by visiting the police station each night to get his free 'doss ticket' (cost of a bed), which was the practice in Scotland at the time. The wheel of fortune started to turn slowly and first he joined the Dumfries Boxing Club and later got a job on a local farm. The job only lasted a short time and once again he was out of work and short of food, which would not do for a future champion, for his fitness was deteriorating. Knowing that road work was essential for any boxer, Paddy set out to walk to England.

His first stop was Carlisle where he pawned some of his clothes to buy food. He was out of luck, however, for the city had nothing to offer. Penrith, Kendal and Lancaster were other stops that could not help the now 'Tramp from Ireland'. His condition, owing to lack of food and sleeping in the open during the winter months, was worsening, so he left Lancaster for Preston. His will to fight gave him a will to live! During his tramp in the rain, on the way to Preston, he noticed a dirty piece of paper in the gutter. On picking it up, he discovered it was an old hymn sheet of 'Safe in the arms of Jesus'. 'This was the first time God spoke to me,' said Paddy, and new life was brought into his aching limbs. He walked on to Manchester, sleeping in hedge bottoms and barns. He was a licensed boxer, so on arrival in the city he went to the northern office of the British Boxing Board of Control and told them he wanted a fight. They directed him to a local gym for a try-out, but he was knocked-out. This was a double blow, for he had to go on living the life he hated, that of scrounging and living in the filthy lodging houses. 'My home in those dark days,' he told me, 'had filthy beds and no sanitary facilities. But I had a roof over my head and it only cost 9d per night.'

While walking the city streets one day, he was told of a boxing booth owner who was setting up a show at Woodhouse Moor Feast at Leeds. He saw the owner, got a job and set off to walk to Leeds. When he arrived on the feast ground the booth owner had not arrived, so he had to spend the night at St George's Crypt, which was during the time of the late Reverend David Robbins. Next day was a happy day for it meant a return to his first love, the boxing ring. It was a very happy Paddy who stood before the crowds at the booth's entrance.

The bright lights were shining and the 'March of the Gladiators' was blaring from the loud speakers. It was not the ideal setting, but it was better than nothing.

Paddy McIlroy – his new name – dipped through the ropes and ground the resin in his corner with the determination of a champion out to retain his title. He fought five times that evening, was announced the winner on five occasions and in the end had won a purse of 5s (25p) - at 1s (5p) a fight. He spent the night sleeping under the governor's trailer. To the boss he was just a meal ticket, but to a Jewish gentleman in the crowd, he was a future champion. The gentleman revealed this to Paddy at a party he gave in his honour the night before he left Leeds. 'You have the best left-hand I have ever seen and if I had the money I would manage you,' said the gentleman.

That was as far as it went, for next day Paddy was on his way with the booth to its next destination, Royston's 1937 spring feast.

As Paddy rode into Royston on the top of the trailer he little knew that the

Jim sells the Salvation Army 'War Cry' newspapers in the smoke-filled working men's clubs.

township would change his life completely within a few years.

The first night in Royston he fought a local welterweight named Burgoine and was disqualified. He thought the fight had been fixed with the referee. The crowd was amused, but he was recalled into the ring later to fight 'Ginger' Mallinson of Barnsley and it went the distance. By the time the feast had ended, Paddy was tired of life and lack of food with the booth and decided to quit. When the show moved on he stayed in Royston and got lodgings in Midland Road and a job pony-driving at New Monckton Colliery.

His first week's wage was more than he had earned for a long time and so, having finished with boxing, he set out to have a good time, a good time which lasted a long time, for he turned into a drunkard, heavy smoker and gambler. They were his pastimes! He visited pubs and clubs in Royston, Barnsley and Staincross every night in the week when he usually had 'one over the eight'. On more than one occasion his pals carried him out of Barnsley fearing he would be arrested for his drunken state.

Films also formed a part of his life and it was during a showing of 'Stanley and Livingstone', the missionary film, that he claimed 'God spoke to me again and I took my first real interest in religion'. Next day, while talking about the film in the pit, a workmate invited him to the Salvation Army and at the weekend he went for a 'bit of fun'. That was 4 February 1940, an important date in Paddy's life, for it transformed the poacher, fighter, tramp, smoker, drinker and gambler into an honest-living citizen.

About his visit to the Citadel, Paddy had this to say:

'I got a real blessing and at once decided to surrender my life to the service and glory of God. The Salvation Army had converted me. No one told me to give up my habits, but as I went out into the street I had no further desire to go on living the life I had followed. I tore up my packet of cigarettes and threw them into the gutter. I was finished with drinking and gambling and determined to live a new life.'

Hearing of his renunciation of his habits and of his new beliefs, his friends just laughed and said he would go mad. 'I would rather go mad in the salvation of the Lord than die mad in sin,' he told them. They said it would only last a few weeks, but 'the power of God has proved greater than the words of men'. He never returned to those habits and served the local Corps as Colour Sergeant, Corps Cadet Guardian, Recruiting Sergeant, Young People's Sergeant Major and Company Guard. When he was converted, he said he would never wear the uniform of the 'Army', but soon he was proud to wear it. There were occasions when he returned to his old haunts in the Staincross area, but it was to distribute the 'Army' publication, the *War Cry*.

During the year of his conversion he met Doris May Goode, of Ryhill, at a youth meeting. They married at Ryhill and seven years later a son, Paul was born, but he died after only nine weeks. Later, they had another son, Philip, who still lives in Ryhill. They were both dedicated (baptised) at the 'Army' Citadel.

Paddy was proud of his new life, in fact so proud that he visited prisons, lodging houses, churches and chapels telling of his salvation. Throughout all the years since he wandered from the 'Emerald Isle', Paddy had a place in his heart for the mother he had never seen, a mother who may have died many years earlier. At Christmas, 1957, his thoughts were with her more than ever. He wanted to contact her, but it seemed out of the question, for his foster parents were now dead. In February 1958, his prayers were answered, for a letter arrived addressed to James McClurg, 22 Churchfields, Ryhill and date stamped 'Portadown County Armagh'. Paddy was surprised, for he had retained the Christian name which was on his birth certificate and McClurg was the name given him by his foster parents. Inside the letter, however, was a link which he had longed for all of his forty-one years. It read: 'Dear James, I am your mother...'

He also learned he had a brother living at Gosport. A most disturbing thing, too, was the fact that the address on the letter was one which he had passed many times when on his holidays in Portadown. He had actually passed his own mother's doorstep and didn't know.

With his wife Doris and son Philip, Paddy went to meet his mother for the first time. She was named Mary Carson and he discovered he had a brother Joe, whom he also later met. Doris recalled:

'His mother had two sons out of wedlock, but eventually married. When they met for the first time, it was an endless embrace with lots of tears. For Paddy it was not the end of his life story, but the beginning of a new one. He now knew his mother, but never knew his father.'

After returning to Ryhill, Paddy made a further visit to his mother, but then she died.

He died in Pinderfields Hospital, Wakefield, on 2 November 1994, aged seventy-seven. A special service was held in the Royston Citadel which he had served for fifty-five years.

Paddy was a Christian gentleman, who never lost his lovely Irish brogue and never lost his love of God.

Lodging House

*E*ver since I can remember there has been a stigma attached to lodging houses. At one period the first 200yd of Doncaster Road, Barnsley, appeared to contain a mystery behind the doors of the lodging houses situated there. Set in the middle of which was the 'I Buy Owt' second-hand shop.

Over the years they disappeared, all but one. The *Model Lodging House*. The postman knew it as number 26 Doncaster Road. The homeless knew it as home. Those who saw 'The Model', early and midway through the century from Doncaster Road, Pontefract Road, or on a passing train, will I am sure have looked in curiosity. They will have said: 'I wonder what it's like inside?'

I had been asking myself the same question since I was a boy, because I can remember the down-trodden men and women in the area, walking

The view of the lodging house from Doncaster Road.

to Charlesworth's pork shop for food and spending winter days in the Gods, the highest balcony in the *Alhambra* cinema, for warmth.

When I left college and became an apprentice plumber, we worked on shops and houses near the lodging house and at one time it was in quarantine for weeks due to a smallpox outbreak. Many people even to this day do not know it existed. The entrance was down a cobbled street between two shops where over the years thousands have been pleased to tread and get a bed for the night, or for half a lifetime.

During my years in journalism I was always on the look-out for unusual features, the lodging house remained in my mind but the owner would not give permission for an interview. Then in 1970 he telephoned to say I could write an article about the three-storey

The sign which Stan Bulmer and myself ignored.

building, where the only secrets were in the minds of the residents. Photographer Stan Bulmer joined me and the first thing we noticed on entering was a sign which read: 'All beds to be paid for by 6.00pm or re-let.' We did not intend staying the night so it did not apply.

The lodging house was registered by Barnsley Corporation to accommodate seventy-four men and on the visit there were nearly sixty present. I first saw the top dormitory which had thirty steel beds with flock mattresses, grey blankets and sheets which were changed twice a week.

Below there was another dormitory for thirty and an extension that would hold a further fourteen. All had bare wood floors which were well swept. There was no furniture or curtains, no lockers for belongings. These were kept in cardboard cartons or suitcases under their beds. Best suits appeared to get special care under sheets of brown paper.

The first resident I met was seventy-year-old Peter McGuire, an Irishman, who had lived there since 1941. He was ill in bed, waiting for an ambulance to take him to hospital for an x-ray after a fall. Before he was carried away, he told me:

> '*I am a bachelor and have been thankful for this place as home. I have no relatives so I shall be happy to spend the rest of my days here. It is cheap and I've plenty of freedom.*'

He died two months later.

Ten women could be accommodated in a separate wing and five were in residence when we called. Again everything was simple but clean and the only decoration was a knitted doll above one bed, probably a prized possession. A large packet of Daz, a hot water bottle and a few possessions in cartons were all that the room contained apart from the steel beds.

The dormitories had to be vacated by 9.00am each day and were then out of bounds until 6.00pm. A bed and roof over one's head cost 4s (40p) per night or £1 2s 6d (£1.12.5p) per week and it was

George Boswell, the mouth-organ player.

Tiger, the lodging house cat near the hearth.

The communal hot-plate with Francis Whitham placing an iron kettle ready for the most important drink - tea.

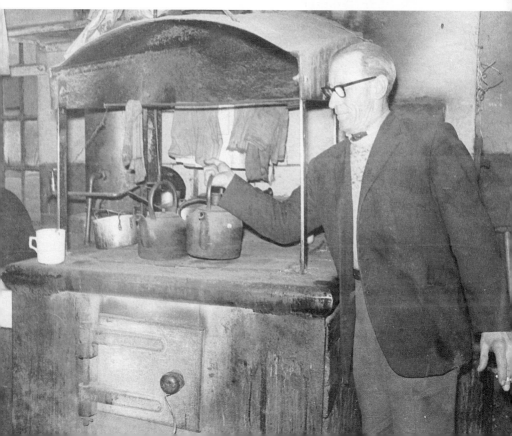

NO ALCOHOLIC DRINKS.... CIDER ETC ALLOWED ON THESE PREMISES!

IN FUTURE ANY ONE IGNORING THIS NOTICE WILL BE TOLD TO LEAVE

One of the men's dormitories.

Two of the numerous signs.

Peter McGuire, awaits the ambulance to take him to hospital. Clothing covered with brown paper hangs on the walls.

claimed to be the cheapest in England. Two hours before they went to bed in winter central heating was switched on in the men's dormitories. For the women there was a paraffin heater in the bedroom and an old Yorkist range in the living area.

The majority of the men worked, but those who did not spent most of their time in the kitchens on the ground floor. There were two sections, each with a communal giant hot plate for cooking which was fired by coal. One was like a giant set-pot which was a feature of every housewife's kitchen in the early part of the century, the other supplied hot water for showers etc.

The only television set was in one of the kitchens where there were nests of lockers in which the lodgers kept their few belongings and cooking equipment. They ate when and what they wanted and the majority had meals inside, although a few ate out at cafes or the Woolworth's snack bar where they could often be seen sitting on the radiators.

During my visit the cooking fumes of kippers, onions, stew, sausage and bacon mingled in the air. The kitchens were the centre of life and while sat around tables, the chaps chatted, dozed or did odd jobs.

George Boswell, at eighty-two, spent his time sat under a window making mouth organs – and playing them. He was a cripple and had been injured by an explosion while serving with the Merchant Navy. He told me:

> *'I joined the Navy in 1908 and rose to the rank of engineer mechanic. But in an explosion in which five people died, I was badly injured and had to leave the service in 1913. I returned to my native Chesterfield, but when my parents died in 1925 I was left without a home. I went on the road and travelled to London, Bedford, St Albans, Barnet, Plymouth and Birmingham before arriving in Barnsley.'*

He walked with the aid of a crutch and seemed a sad figure. He pulled from his pocket a brown paper bag which contained his proudest possession, a home-made mouth organ. He smiled and put it to his lips to play 'Sons of the Sea' to perfection and the other chaps in the kitchen sang and hummed the tune.

Sitting in a corner quietly, no doubt thinking about better times, was seventy-two-year-old Maria Coles Adams, who was quick to emphasise that 'Coles' was her Christian name. She had lived there for twenty years. She kept her money and valuable possessions strapped round her waist. Born in South Wales, she then moved to Sunderland and when her house there was condemned, she could not settle in her new home. Her husband died in 1921 and she headed for Leeds from where, after a short spell, she moved to Barnsley. She rarely went out and spent her time making tea or 'talking to myself'. She was a well known figure scrounging around the market stalls. She had five sons and a daughter, but she had not seen any of them for twenty years. 'I often think about them,' she said. Francis Witham, at 53, had made it his home after domestic trouble. 'While ever there is a building I will stay here,' he told me.

With so many folks about the stone floors could soon become slippery. Scattered sand prevented this and also proved to be an effective cleaning agent. The floor was swept every day and twice a year in September and April, the walls of the kitchens were treated with lime wash blue.

The women had their own kitchen with an open range, sinks and a three-piece suite. Plastic roses decorated the table and pictures of singer Tom Jones decorated the door.

Mabel Goulding, at 67, had lived there for twelve years, moving from a Sheffield lodging house for a change of surroundings. She was parted from her husband, had four children, but only knew the whereabouts of one. She read widely from Shakespeare to Sherlock Holmes, went to bed at eight and her only possessions were cooking utensils, a bucket and 'Tiger', the lodging house cat.

Another woman, who would not give her name, said:

'I would not like to leave. I have relatives, but they never come to see if I am dead or alive. There are better people in here than outside. So many people criticise the place, but to us it is a good home.'

There was a code amongst the residents and they were quick to help anyone in need. Strangers arriving always got a welcome. A person wanting accommodation had to register at the office-cum-shop. If it was a person who had previously been banned for trouble making, then they were not admitted. If their record was good there was a bed, and if they had no money they were given a form to take to the Social Security office where, if they were satisfied, the bed fee was paid. Known malingerers were sent on their way.

The main door was locked at 11.00pm, although a compulsory night-watchman would admit any residents who had been on shift work or were expected late.

Returning to the little shop, it provided a few of life's necessities, such as tea bags, which produced two pints of tea for a penny, vinegar concentrate at 3d and 'Indian Brandee' for stomach upsets. At the time I feared what would happen to the people I met if the place

How things had changed fifteen years later... the women's bed and wash room.

closed. It had a purpose, an essential purpose to the life of Barnsley. The stigma of the past had gone and although the folks I met had sad hearts they did appear to be content with their lot and it provided community life for those who felt they were too old to mix with society, or still cherished their freedom.

For me, the mystery unfolded and I felt privileged to have been allowed by the owners to visit 'The Model'.

My final feeling and comment was:

'To all those who have a home, no matter how simple, for God's sake cherish it.'

In April 1985, fifteen years later, I was invited back to see the transformation that was taking place to rid the facility of its 'doss house' image. It was a £100,000-plus renovation, the first major change since it became a lodging house in 1870, before which it was a beer warehouse.

The lodging house was now run by James McNicholas, assisted by his son Bernard. They had been told by Barnsley Environmental Health Department, that the premises would have to close if improvements were not made over a five-year period .

When I had first visited, it was a regulation that eighteen inches of the wall had to be covered in creosote and the rest lime washed. The new dormitories had lowered ceilings, walls plastered, strip lights, floor coverings, gas convectors and new beds.

There were new toilets and wash rooms and even a washing room with electric washers and gas dryers. The huge hot plates had gone, being replaced by gas cookers. Also replaced was the lime-wash decor, this time by magnolia emulsion.

James McNicholas and his son had done a super job and Philip Hunt, at the time the council's Central Area Environmental Officer, told me:

'Lodging house keepers have to be registered annually and we do regular inspections. I was concerned in 1982 that the time was approaching when, if major works were not carried out, we would have to consider not re-registering. But that would have left 60 people homeless. A schedule of works was prepared and the owners agreed to it. There is a need for this type of accommodation and we now have a properly equipped and well run place for years to come.'

The residents and owners were happy, but over the years new legislation put pressure on the management. On 27 November 1998 'The Model' served its last twelve tenants and closed its doors. Since 1870 it had been a major part of Barnsley life.

The homeless are often forgotten people and such unfortunates are thought to exist only in the big cities, living in cardboard boxes under the arches or in streets.

Barnsley has had its share of homelessness over the years and again I was privileged in 1996 to be asked by Canon George Nairn-Briggs, the Bishop of Wakefield's Adviser for Social Responsibility, to support the English Churches Housing Group who had transformed the former Race Street Baths into Holden House, a unique-supported housing project for the homeless.

It provides accommodation for forty-four men and women in shared and self-contained accommodation. The level of support and services reflects the complexity of issues tenants may have to address, ranging from mental illness and physical disability to bankruptcy, family breakdown and abuse. I obtained some finance towards equipping this superb facility.

The facilities at Holden House are a long way from those offered by The Model Lodging House, but it is a sad reflection on society that the same problems persist.

My feelings are still the same, homes should be cherished and it is not until they are lost that they are fully appreciated.

Morganeering

Morgan three-wheelers have a place in my motoring memories which stem from the time I thought such a vehicle would join the Booker household.

One winter's day I went with my dad to Skelmanthorpe where a three-wheeler was for sale. We went for a test run and the noise of the huge J.A.P. V twin engine was incredible. I could see the giant chain driving the rear wheel, while water dripped over me through the canvas top. The price was £120, but the deal was never made.

Reading everything I could lay hands on about Morgans, I was inspired by this all-British product, particularly the mechanical simplicity of the cars. A love affair with Morgans started and I began saving money for a four-wheeler. In 1965, as today, there was a waiting list, so I put a £20 deposit on a Four-Four model at the dealer, Bolton of Halifax, for a car costing £1,300. Dealerships changed and the passage of the three-year wait was helped by my daily reading of a chapter from 'Morgan, Last of the Real Sports Cars' by Gregory Houston Bowden. It was like having a Gideon Bible at my bedside.

When the car was eventually delivered the price was £3,110, but I had become part of a motoring legend. Morgan owners, no matter what status they hold in life, are among the most friendly I have met. Meet a fellow Morganeer and you make a friend for life.

For over twenty-five years I owned Morgans, two Four-Four four-seaters and three Plus-Fours, one with a Fiat engine and the others Ford or Rover. Although not British, the Fiat engine was the best. Derek Cook, of the D.C. Cook motoring empire, bought my first and used it for taking guests to the christening of his son, while others went to various parts of the country, including one to a doctor at the famous Brooklands racing circuit.

There was never a problem selling a Morgan and I always gave the buyer a bottle of wine to celebrate their joining the Morganeers and they gave me a bottle of Malvern water with which to christen my new car. The cars never let me down mechanically, but I lost a few exhaust systems, which were prone to rust from the inside due to limited use. There was a time when we had to motor from the A1, with my wife Freda holding the silencer in the front seat and our daughter Julie holding the rest of the system across the rear seats. That's why Morgan drivers are like the pioneers of motoring.

My first Morgan in 1976, which was later bought by motor magnate Derek Cook.

Audi's Phil Stein decided to launch the 100 from the lovely Cotswold village of Broadway. The Morgan is made for such beautiful countryside, so I decided to travel in the car and take it to the factory in Pickersleigh Road, Malvern, for a service while testing the German car.

Again, it was the start of a long friendship with the owner of the Morgan Motor Company, Peter Morgan and later his son Charles. Many services were carried out at the factory and such visits became a holiday. We would stay overnight at the Abbey Hotel and next morning at 8.00am I would drive the car to the factory and then walk back across the hills for breakfast, after which we would visit the town and walk in the Malvern Hills until about 4.30pm before making the journey home. With a Morgan motoring is a joy.

Over the years I became an ambassador for the marque, taking many motoring writers to the factory, among whom were the heads of Volkswagen and Mercedes-Benz who also became owners of Morgan cars.

These were my impressions for a *Chronicle* article after my first factory visit:

'*There is nothing posh about the Morgan works at Malvern Link, Worcestershire. The car is made at the world's oldest car factory. An undistinguished place, with a red brick frontage and the letters MM over the door. Nearby is a more modern sign carrying the word*

Morgan.'

Arriving at the factory, I was met by a chap sitting on a box at the main door eating corned beef sandwiches. 'It's time for lunch,' he said. 'But take a look around.' In the service area an apprentice was preparing his lunch – two slices of bread placed on a shovel which he had pushed inside the coke stove.

The managing director, Peter Morgan, son of the founder, H.F.S. Morgan, has an office a few yards from the stores. It is not palatial, in fact the walls are made of tongued-and-grooved boarding carrying many coats of paint, covered with photographs of Morgan sporting feats, including winning Le Mans. Peter Morgan is a proud and friendly man and was only too pleased to tell me about his company, where sons usually follow fathers and are trained in all aspects of sports car making.

'I usually find if a lad lasts a year with the company, he will stay a lifetime. There is a good management-worker relationship,' he said.

Works chief Jim Goodall is also a director and had been with Morgans, like his father, for over forty years. Sales director Derek Day has been there for thirty years. Over the years Derek and I have

The Morgan I sold in 1996 to a Harley Street specialist. It was a gem.

become great friends, meeting on factory visits and at motor shows. He retired in 1997.

After the stores comes the despatch bay, where cars are prepared for despatch to the world's markets. It is in this bay where the individual requirements of the future owners are installed because a Morgan buyer can have the car built just as he likes. On one visit cars awaited King Hussein of Jordan and King Carlos of Spain.

Italian buyers seem to prefer two-tone bodywork, while the Australians go for red and red wire wheels. Some cars are trimmed with hand-tooled leather – they are a sight to make the heart thump. While the outward appearance of Morgans has changed little, there have been many under-the-skin improvements to meet safety and emission control regulations.

In the next building each Monday morning rows of small trestles are set out, enough to carry the week's production. On these are mounted the steel chassis frames, to which are fitted the brake, clutch and accelerator pedals, front suspension frame and handbrake lever. Then the chassis is carried to another section where brake pipes, the engine (lifted by a man-operated pulley), the bulkhead, steering column, shock absorbers, springs and wheels are fitted.

There is no automation and porters are called to push the 'car' to the next work bay where the wooden subframe, usually Belgian ash, is fitted. One worker showed me a bullet which had come from a piece of wood.

> *'That was from a weapon used in the First World War and got embedded in the Belgian-grown tree. We get a lot and they often damage the saw blades,'* he said.

Before the wood frame is put to rest on the chassis, a damp-proof course is glued to the frame, just like the ones used in house building. That prevents rising damp getting to the frame and wooden floor.

The wood door frames are individually made for each car before the 'pushers' come along and take the developing vehicle to the body shop where the wheel arches are fitted. The body shop is the most important part of the factory and where the majority of the men work.

With shears, they cut out the sheet steel – or aluminium – for the body panels and in true sheet metal worker fashion beat the panels by hand to fit each part of the body. It takes about two days to complete the panels for a car.

From there the car goes to the chaps who fit the wings and cowl and then to the bonnet-maker who cuts the forty bonnet louvres with an old-fashioned fly press – the same piece of equipment which was installed before the First World War.

The radiator grille is also made by hand, each chrome strip being individually soldered into place. In the paint shop great care is taken in preparing the body, then the wiring harness is fitted and the car moves forward to the newest part of the factory, the trim shop.

Sat at machines that Singers never thought still existed, women cut and trim carpets, seat covers, hoods and tonneau covers. Nothing is pre-cut and put into stock, everything being made to match every press stud on each car.

Sitting on a girder in the collection bay is a stuffed owl. His task is to put fear into any birds who try to fly inside and leave their droppings on the polished cars.

On my visit, just the Plus Eight with a Rover engine and Four-Four two and four seaters with a Ford engine models were being made.

My relationship with the factory over the years has been such that when I have telephoned, they have recognised my voice immediately. Imagine that at the big car factories.

Sir John Harvey-Jones tried his best to get the Morgan family to change things, but he failed. His famous 'Trouble Shooter' programme did not harm the company, he just gained the marque more popularity and added a further year to the six-year waiting list! Walking in Harrogate, I recognised Sir Harvey and we chatted about

The factory banner that says it all.

They think of everyone at Malvern Link, or the waiting list could mean a bike rather than a Morgan.

the programme. I told him I did not like his comments and ideas of the Morgan Car Company. His reply:

> *'Well, they think I'm a wally and I think they are wallies. But they are a great company'.*

I told him there was more to life than making money. The Morgan family were happy, the workforce were happy and the customers were more than happy. What was wrong with that philosophy? He went on his way without making any comment.

There is a love-hate relationship with a Morgan, but the majority love them. There is something really special about this, the last of the real sports cars and once out of the car you know you have ridden in one. There is an impression on your backside – a kind of numbness which lasts for about an hour.

As far as Morgan cars are concerned, an extra wheel was added in 1936, but the suspension at the front – the sliding-pillar type – is just as it was in 1910, yes, even in the year 2000. An American enthusiast told me:

> *'Riding in a Morgan is like sitting bare-bottomed on a coal scuttle and bouncing down a flight of stairs.'*

I don't reckon it is as bad as that, but you certainly remember a ride in a Morgan. It is a thrilling experience, away from the cosy interior of the modern car where if a draught can be felt coming from any direction, the owner will dash off to the dealer and complain. It is a car where a few water leaks in the cockpit are accepted with joy.

It is motoring adventure at its best. If you feel depressed, a ride in a Morgan will not only bring colour to your cheeks (the facial kind), but it will also make you feel good to be alive. It is different... it is British.

During summer runs one often meets older motorists who want to inspect the car.

'I once had a Morgan three-wheeler, never any trouble. I didn't think they still made 'em', is usually their comment.

They all smile, because they have happy memories.

A friend, Jayne Walkden, who was expecting a baby, asked for a

With Peter Morgan on the company stand at the International Motor Show, Birmingham.

ride in the car. 'I want my baby to ride in a Morgan before it is born' she said. The baby was born on Bonfire Day. The bumpy ride did not bring about a premature birth.

While visiting Howarth I was surrounded by some thirty French teenagers on a tour of Britain. For over an hour, through an interpreter, I had to explain how the car was made and then they all wanted their photographs taken alongside it.

'Bridget Bardot set the style in France with her Morgan,' said their leader. *'We love them and in the South of France many holidaymakers hire Morgans.'*

But you also get the funny types who will describe the car as 'Noddy's car'. Yet there are thousands whose hearts belong to Morgan.

Whether I am at home or abroad I always find people who want to know about the Morgan. Some, whom I meet several times a year, always ask, 'How's the Morgan ?' It is as though the car is a member of the family...and so it is.

Why then has the Morgan stood the test of time so well when many other small car manufacturers have gone out of business? It is built by dedicated workers and is a car that has had very few styling changes. The most obvious was probably the change from the flat radiator to the present 'showing its teeth', more streamlined style.

In 1993 I bought a Plus-Four in British Racing Green, with red leather interior and chrome wire wheels. Three years later I sold it to a Harley Street specialist. The only reason I parted with it was that it took too long to erect the hood and I was getting too old for a soaking by rain when caught in a storm.

There are always some regrets in life and losing the Morgan was one. Like so many other drivers, my motoring heart will always belong to Morgan.

The heart-strings pulled so tight that in June 1999, a Morgan was back in the family. Another Plus-Four, but, this time, in Aston Martin silver, with blue leather and chrome wheels. A pilot with Airtours had waited six years for the car, but then it was not to his liking; his loss was my gain!

My romance with Morgan continues.

Wood Smoke

A wartime evacuee from London called Geoff stimulated my interest in the Scout Movement. He talked about adventurous things such as the game British Bulldog, tracking in the countryside, building bridges with poles and rope and cooking at camp on an open fire.

There was little to excite young boys during the war years, but Scouting seemed to provide enough activities to brighten life. I was only ten years old, but, to join the Scouts, one had to be eleven. Geoff was a member of the St Helen's Group which met in a wooden church building, and the Scoutmaster was a Church Army officer. On a Thursday evening I gave my wrong age to join and was accepted, but only stayed a few weeks when I moved to St Barnabas Group which had a 'Scout Hut', in Mottram Street, Barnsley. It was a poor building, but was well organised. My first patrol leader, Colin Wegg, had a patrol second called Partridge, but he was nicknamed 'Parrot'.

We had monthly church parades to St Barnabas Church in Old Mill Lane, but as yet I had no uniform, just a neckerchief with the famously called 'woggle'. One needed clothing coupons for uniform and there was always a shortage at the local Scout shop, Fletcher and Frankland, in New Street. There was a waiting list for the famous khaki felt Scout hat that protected one from the rain and was handy to carry water and fan camp fires. A damp cloth and hot iron kept the brim firm.

The 39th Barnsley (Monk Bretton) troop was nearer home and this troop was kept alive by Ethel Moyer and Len Norris in the church hall. The troop's pre-war headquarters in the old Church School had been taken over by the Home Guard. We had no flags and no camping gear because this had all been put into storage by the Scouts who had been called up to serve with the Armed Forces. There was no overnight camping because of the black-out so we had day trips to Notton Park, which was an exciting adventure. There were lots of pine trees, a stream and trees in which we made houses, but we still lacked equipment.

I was invested a Scout by Len Norris in the Church Hall and can still remember the ceremony and the promise I made. It meant I got my first Scout badge.

The group went back into the old school for a short time, but then had to move out when it was taken over by Green Monk Products, famous for making the 'Sooty' xylophone. We then moved into the cottage in the Welfare Park with James Nathaniel (he always emphasised this name) Winterbottom, who returned from the RAF, as Group Scout Leader. We were cramped and met in the small front room where we also played football. The goal was the fire grate. We got together some items of equipment and later Don Davis became assistant Scoutmaster.

There were no cars available to us so everything for camp had to be carried or taken on a handcart. We had campsites at Silverwood Camp, Silkstone and at High Green. Notton Wood was never returned to the Scouts after the war, because much of the land had been cultivated for the war effort. Silverwood was purchased in 1948 out of a legacy left to the Barnsley Scout Association by Miss Elizabeth Silverwood. The name 'Silverwood' was given to the camp to commemorate the donor and because of the abundance of silver birch trees in the surrounding woods.

The site had been used for the training of the 1st and 2nd Barnsley Battalions in the 1914 to 1918 war and was covered with concrete blocks on which huts had been erected and concrete areas which had been used for ablutions. We helped to develop the site and our Rover Crew would stay in a woodcutter's shed among the pine trees. On one side was a store and on the other a room with an open fire. We either cooked on that fire or built an outside oven and cooked there. We built a chapel in the wood and the Vicar of Silkstone, Father Derek Birch would come and celebrate Holy Communion there.

It was when the camp Tilley lamp finally went out at bed times that we realised that splinters from silver birch were luminous. We had chopped wood for the fire leaving the splinters on the floor, but when we relit the light they disappeared.

By that time Jim Winterbottom had secured a former wartime decontamination centre in Board Yard, High Street, Monk Bretton, as a more permanent headquarters and we ripped out the showers and built an open fireplace. It was a very homely place and we spent many years there, eventually turning the group into Yorkshire's first Air Scout Unit. To gain recognition we had to maintain high standards and were inspected annually by an officer from RAF Finningley.

Scouting became very much part of my life and I was inspired by Lord Baden-Powell's *Scouting for Boys* and *Rovering to Success*. I thought if the world followed the inspiration of those books along

Hands on hips interview with Chief Scout Lord Maclean at Hesley Wood Camp.

with the Bible what a wonderful place it would be.

Raymond Brockbank, home from war service, became a Scoutmaster with responsibility for Senior Scouts. We had purple epaulettes and I remember getting mine from Hendre Heckenroth, a French interpreter at the first World Jamboree after the war. He became a Roman Catholic priest in Aix-en-Provence and I have often looked for his name on church notice boards when I have been in that part of the world.

From Senior Scouts to Rover Crew, we had great times, especially when we helped to build the swimming pool at Silverwood Camp. There was no aggregate available in those days so we collected stones by hand to mix with the concrete. With 'Skip' Lines, of Wombwell, as leader, we also worked, winter and summer, building the first Silverwood Lodge.

The inspirational leader of Scouting in Barnsley was Captain Howard Walker, a local solicitor who, over the years, became a great friend and supporter of all I tried to do for Scouting. He became County Commissioner after Sir Harold West, who wore 'long' shorts three inches below the top of his stockings! He too did much for Scouting in South Yorkshire.

As well as visiting Silverwood, we had annual camps at Coniston in the Lake District and on the East Yorkshire coast. Yewdale Farm was the Coniston base and we hired Goody's coal lorry on a Thursday to take all our gear to Cudworth railway station where it was loaded into a goods carriage. On one occasion I even took my *Chronicle* scooter. When we arrived at the site all the equipment would be in the field waiting.

On the way to the site we would call at the Coniston Co-op stores to collect supplies. They were great camps, and when I made a nostalgic visit to the site in June 2000, I discovered it had been owned by children's writer Beatrix Potter.

As a Pressman, I covered Scouting in South Yorkshire for nearly forty years, being public relations adviser to the county and working with several Chief Scouts on their visits north. I also played a part in the first Patrol Leaders' Council, held at Hesley Wood County Camp, where in the 1940s we had been the first Scouts to camp.

In July 1945, I was in charge of publicity when Chief Scout Lord Rowallan, flew into Silverwood by helicopter to open officially the

With Scouts from around the world at the 1957 Jubilee Jamboree at Sutton Coldfield.

swimming pool we had helped to create.

The Monk Bretton Scout Group thrived and it was the envy of the county. In our Rover Crew we had Colin Wroe, Ernest Horbury, Peter Scrivener, Bill Hawcroft, Eric Graham, Adrian Eggleston, Dick France, Ernest Williams, Ernest Forrest and Geoff Roystone. We all worked at Silverwood when Don Jennings was warden.

When the RAF visited, Eric Graham and Ernest Forrest always arranged a three-course dinner, prepared with our limited cooking facilities. One Sunday they overloaded the electric cooker to such an extent that it cut off all the power in High Street. At the events we had a licensed bar and it was manned by Ernest, wearing a bow tie and bright waistcoat. At the time we were the only Scout group with an account at a brewery.

Group Scout Leader Jim died suddenly, just as we were told we would have to find a new home, and I was appointed Group Leader. The Board Yard building was to be demolished to make way for housing. We searched the area and even considered buying the former West Green Club, but it was away from the centre of the village. The group had been founded in 1933 and looked as though it would have to be disbanded, but a wonderful parents' committee – one of the best I have known – set about raising money for a permanent headquarters. For nearly two years we had to hold our meetings around a snooker table in the Miners' Welfare Hall but we managed to survive.

Ernest Forrest, Jack Woffinden, Eric Graham and Harold Clarke were dedicated Scout trainers and members of the public also gave us their financial support. Frank Cooper, head of Ideal Homes, who were building a large residential estate in Monk Bretton, succumbed to my pressures and offered a large plot of land off Rotherham Road for just £25. Our dream was nearly realised, but we were still £1,600 short. I decided to apply to the Department of Education and Science for a grant which was available through a 1938 Act, but I hit a stumbling block when it went before Barnsley Council. No progress was made even though all I wanted was their endorsement of the application. John Dossett, a Liberal councillor, was asked to investigate and his efforts resulted in the endorsement eventually being given.

When I approached the local Member of Parliament, Roy Mason, for help he certainly gave us every support and the next I heard was that a cheque for £1,600 had arrived. We worked every spare hour preparing the site and lining the concrete building. Eric Lawton, Jack Woffinden, Eric Graham, Bob Elborough, Harold Clarke, Bruce

The Air Scout Group that met weekly around a snooker table with, seated centre, Tito Chian Wong, Chief Scout of Peru.

Myself, Tito and Field Commissioner John Wolfe, when the Peruvian made a return visit.

Whincup, Ben Peaker, John Hazelhurst and John Taylor did the building work, while our wives raised the money.

There were never any arguments and everyone enjoyed what they were doing, an essential factor in church and charity work. When the new headquarters was officially opened by Howard Walker, the County Commissioner who had let me borrow £250 to pay the final bill, it was named as a Scout Centre, rather than the traditional Scout Hut.

Scouting is the world's greatest voluntary youth organisation and again my travels brought me international connections. The first came at the 1957 International Jamboree, Indaba and Moot at Sutton Coldfield, when, along with Dick France, I was part of the Press Corps. There I made links with Canada, Israel, Holland and France.

My biggest foreign link came when I was group leader and we were based in the Miners' Hall. We had the second biggest Scout group in Yorkshire and this led Field Commissioner John Wolfe, who was helping with our building project, to ask if I would allow the Chief Scout of Peru, Tito Chian Wong, to spend time with the group.

Tito was visiting the UK as part of his training and since that time we have enjoyed a wonderful relationship with his wife Betty, daughter Bettina and son Papu. He was based in Lima and I have always tried to help his Scouts in the shanty towns of the city. When a video of Scouting was made available, I thought it would stimulate the interest of young Peruvians. I sent him a copy but it was never

Peruvian friends, Christmas 1999 - Stefan, Bettina, Papu, Tito and Betty with family pet.

received by Tito.

After a year he investigated the disappearance of the tape and was told it had been confiscated by Customs because they saw the film of Baden-Powell in his war days and Scouts marching. They believed I was transmitting messages on terrorism. This may also explain why some of my other items had not reached their destination.

Tito is a true and dedicated Scouter, former professional footballer, engineer and travel agent. A wonderful Scouting friend.

After stepping down from Scout leadership, I maintained links with Scouting, working in public relations and with membership of the Scout Fellowship. Our daughter, Julie, who visited Tito and his family and toured Peru, went on to maintain the family Scouting link by working as a designer at Gilwell Park, the International Training Centre and Baden-Powell House in London.

There are some things in life that touch our emotions and one of mine is seeing the Scout and Guide flags being carried down a church aisle to the altar. I also love to hear the following Scout Hymn sung on St George's Day to the tune of 'Abide with Me'.

Now as I start upon my chosen way
In all I do, my thoughts, my work, my play,
Grant, as I promise, courage new to me
To be the best, the best that, I can be.

Help me to keep my honour shining bright.
May I be loyal in the hardest fight.
Let me be able for my task and then
To earn a place among my fellow men.

Open my eyes to see the things I should,
That I may do my daily turn of good.
Let me be ready, waiting for each need
To keep me clean in thought and word and deed.

So, as I journey on my chosen way,
In all I do, my thoughts, my work, my play,
Grant, as I promise, courage new to me
To be the best, the best that, I can be.

That London evacuee will never know that he introduced me to one of the major involvements of my life.

Mike the Bike

In the 1950s the *Chronicle* had strong opposition from another weekly paper, the *South Yorkshire Times*, which was also family-owned and was based at Mexborough. *The Times* sold more than 50,000 copies a week and covered every district where the *Chronicle* operated. The *Chronicle* sold 42,000 copies a week.

Covering the Royston district one Monday morning I started my calls in Station Road with Grace Berry, who was secretary of the Co-op Guild and the Darby and Joan Club. It was outside her house that I met a new junior reporter from the *Times*. He was on a bike with low drop handlebars just like the machine I had always wanted. He introduced himself as Michael Parkinson and said he was being trained by Stain Bristow of Grimethorpe. From that morning we developed a good working relationship as we both covered the mining villages.

A teenage Michael Parkinson (under the light bulb), with a group of Barnsley journalists.

I had a motorcycle, so Mike would leave his bike and ride pillion. The day we met he had been on the road since 6.00am, taking copy to Grimethorpe and then back to Cudworth railway station, for transit to his head office at Mexborough.

At that time newspapermen were portrayed in films as slick guys who chain-smoked, drank heavily and had trilby hats worn at a slant so we bought trilby hats with broad brims edged with braid, but on a motorcycle, they blew off into the hedge bottoms. We got the hats from Westnedge's store in Royston and returned there to find a remedy. Harold Westnedge sold us two yards of knicker elastic which we tied into bands and put them over the hats and under our chins. The problem was instantly solved.

Riding pillion relieved Mike's tired legs. We would ride over fields and footpaths to get news stories. We ate lunch early, about 11.00am, at the Railway canteen or *Sylvia's Caf* in Midland Road. It usually consisted of treacle pudding and custard rinsed down with a pot of tea. If I was unable to take him to Cudworth, Mike would catch Rowe's double-decker bus, which ran every two hours. Once we had collected our daily news we would then do a swap, but were always looking to scoop each other when the other's back was turned. We never knew until the Friday who had managed an exclusive story.

Michael seemed to live on his cycle and he became known as *Mike the Bike*. He enjoyed covering sport in those days, especially West Riding League cricket and Nelson League soccer. Every Saturday night he would be out on his bike, collecting match reports.

One duty we always shared was collecting obituaries. In those days there were no chapels of rest and when we called at the houses, the deceased would be laid out on coffin-shaped boards hired from the undertaker. They would be in a room without a fire, usually behind a clothes-horse over which was draped a white cotton sheet. The sheets would have been stored in a drawer for years to await the laying out, usually by a woman from the neighbourhood.

After getting family details, we were often asked to view the body. Out of respect, we always commented: 'He looks well.' We requested a photograph of the deceased and, when I was freelancing, it meant an extra 2s 6d (12.5p). If there was only one photograph, Michael would often let me take it to help boost my wage which some weeks was only 7s 6d (35.5p) and that was at the age of twenty!

We of course also covered local fires. At that time Royston had a retained fire brigade, which was based in a large shed in High Street. The firemen were called by a siren that sounded over the town. One morning when we were on our rounds, the siren sounded and a few minutes later the fire engine appeared on Midland Road. Station Officer Paling saw us and told the driver to stop to allow us to travel with them to the scene of the fire.

On another occasion, we went to Monckton Row where a fire had destroyed a terraced house. It was in a long row of cottages only a few yards from the pit, coke and chemical plant. The children were preparing for bonfire night and were afraid their 'Bunnywood' would be stolen by gangs. One family decided to store the wood in the front room, but in the early hours one youngster got out of bed, put a match to it and burnt down the house.

Michael went to do his National Service, in part during the Suez Crisis and then for a short time returned to the *Times*. I managed to get him a job in the reporters' room at the *Chronicle* from where, after a few months, he moved to a Doncaster evening paper and then the world became his writing domain.

His fame as a first-class journalist in newspapers and on television brought many requests for my story of our working background. The first came in October 1971, when the *Radio Times* came to the area to interview his friends and school mates. Among these was 'Skinner' Normanton, whom he had immortalised in his famous *Sunday Times* articles. The feature covered four pages and included Michael's neighbours, the Shentons, with son Mike, now the *Chronicle's*

Stan Bristow and myself join him on This is Your Life *television set at the New London Theatre, Drury Lane*

The personalities line-up at the end of the show.

advertising manager.

In August 1978, a call came from Thames Television asking for an interview. They came to my home and swore me to secrecy, for they were planning a programme in the *This is Your Life* series on Michael Parkinson and wanted me to take part. They took details of our working days and then sent a camera crew with an unusual request. They had obtained a BSA motorcycle similar to the one we had used on our news rounds and they wanted me to ride it around the villages. I was a little worried because I had not been on a motorcycle for over thirty years and when they said they had found the machine in a museum my worry intensified.

They brought the bike in a furniture van with a ten-man crew and took film in Royston and around Cudworth railway station. I managed to keep my balance on the bike, even with Stan Bristow on the pillion, but then came another suggestion from the producer, Jack Crawshaw, who asked: 'We would like you to ride the bike on the theatre stage.' This time I said: 'No.' I thought the show would be ruined if it failed to kick-start in the wings. They were also advised to drain the petrol from the tank – knowing what old bikes are like. Instead the BSA was positioned behind the show's sliding doors and I sat there, sounded the horn, with Stan again on the pillion.

The big filming day was 18 October and I was met at Euston

The day I employed Mike for a special BBC2 radio programme.

The night that Mike and Dickie Bird were listeners while I spoke at the local newsagents' dinner.

The Barnsley trio with newsagent dinner guests at Ardsley House Hotel.

railway station by a driver carrying a Thames TV card. He took me to the *New London* theatre to join others taking part and after lunch we had a rehearsal with a stand-in for presenter Eammon Andrews. We were allocated dressing rooms. I shared with Dickie Bird and we were asked not to wear anything red because it caused a blur on the screen. If we wanted to go to the toilet we would be escorted by 'Angela'. Dickie refused. 'No woman's taking me to the toilet,' he said, and held on for two hours. The idea was to keep voices away from Michael's dressing room so he would not recognise them before the show.

While we had tea, Eammon Andrews and Michael's sons, Andrew, Nicholas and Michael, set off down the Thames on a cruiser to the family home. They went up the garden path and met Michael in the kitchen with the famous big red book containing aspects of his career.

He agreed to go on the programme and a call was made to the theatre to tell everyone that the plans would go ahead. The Parkinson family then left for the *New London* theatre where we were waiting and Michael's life was presented before an audience of nearly 1,000. The show was one of the first to be pre-recorded and Thames Television did this because on one occasion the personality had refused to appear.

First to face the camera were his wife, Mary, herself a television personality and his mother, Freda, who at one time lived in Moorland Terrace, Cudworth. His uncle, Jim Seacroft, and his wife Madge, were then introduced. Jim was a former Cudworth Urban District Council official.

Cricket personalities Geoff Boycott and Dickie Bird were filmed at Shaw Lane cricket ground where they recalled their days in the same team as 'Parky'. Boycott also threw a cricket ball on the stage – but the inner-ball had been removed to avoid any accidents.

The man who gave Michael his first stage chance, Lionel Mosley, a former youth leader, also recalled the days of the village's famous one-act plays. Other sporting personalities were George Best, who had flown from California and Alvin Kallicharran, the West Indies cricket captain.

The world of show business was represented by Petula Clark, Jimmy Tarbuck, Ronnie Scott, Marion Montgomery, the Harry Stoneham Five and Robert Powell, who played the part of Jesus in the film 'Jesus of Nazareth'. He was filmed in America. There was also Scottish personality Billy Connolly, who commented on the 'Barnsley Body Builders' - a huge plate of chips - and Russell Harty.

Journalism was represented by Robin Esser, of the *London Evening News*, who served with Michael as a press officer in Suez and Tony Howard, a *Times* columnist.

Behind the backdrop for the show we simply lined up ready to meet the camera. A make-up artist put a few touches to our faces and Jimmy Tarbuck played 'Singing in the Rain' on a portable organ – it made Dickie want to go to the toilet.

After the show, we all enjoyed a buffet supper while the programme was played back. Then we were taken to the *Clive Hotel*, Hampstead. Shortly after going to my room to unpack there came a knock at the door. It was an unhappy Dickie who said:

> *'Will tha eva look at mi room, there's noor bed. Ahv been in hotels all ovver t'world, but nevver one like this!'*

Off I went to find that, instead of a bed, there was a divan with a brown cover. Because it had not been made-up like a bed, Dickie thought it was just a settee. I made up the bed for him.

The next morning *Daily Mail* columnist Nigel Dempster, leaked the show by referring to Geoff Boycott staying at a London hotel.

When Michael was starring in Australia, I received a telephone call at 4.00am from the *Melbourne Truth* newspaper who had heard about our working exploits which always seemed to involve a grave digger. They asked for photographs and a full-page feature appeared with the headline

'Grave digger's low down for Parky...digging up his roots.'

They said:

'It's not hard to see how Parky learned the graveside manner he uses to such devastating effect on his chat show guests - although the technique had admittedly been refined.'

Whenever he was in the news, I would get calls for a comment and one in 1998 came from Carol Smillie who wanted details for her *People* programme.

Michael Parkinson has come a long way since riding pillion on my motorcycle and working in the pit villages around Barnsley.

A true Yorkshire lad, he has changed little, in spite of interviewing the world's most famous and glamorous personalities for print and screen. He also has a good memory, for when we meet he often recalls the period when he fancied Kath, the cook at Royston Railway canteen. She made excellent pies and sponge puddings, but he was more fascinated by her bust than her culinary skills.

This is Your Life again invited me to appear on the show for old music mate Stan Richards.

That was recorded at the Yorkshire Television studios in Leeds.

I was deemed to have acquired so much experience at these shows that when the *Chronicle* celebrated its 125th Anniversary with a big birthday party in the Drill Hall, Barnsley, lined with drapes, I was prevailed upon to present *This is Your Life, Chronicle*-style. It featured getting the *Chronicle* chairman, Sir Nicholas Hewitt and his brother and deputy chairman, Timothy Hewitt, into a galvanised bath in the centre of the floor. Later, the *Chronicle* bought the Drill Hall.

Council Affairs

A ttending local council and education committee meetings forms a major part of provincial newspaper reporting and having to work five nights a week is routine.

From the 1940s until the 1980s, most meetings were held in the evening and the number increased when some councils made their committee meetings open to the public. These meetings were a great source of stories and it was necessary to cover parish, urban, rural and county council meetings, plus school managers, governors and education executive meetings. All the bodies had dedicated unpaid members and some were real characters.

The first meeting I attended was Ryhill Parish Council. I had never heard of the village, never mind what was expected from me. Chief reporter Vivian Turner, although a brilliant journalist, was always under the influence of drink when he gave out jobs for the evening. He only knew the journey from his Dodworth Road digs to the office, magistrates' court and a pub at Graham's Orchard, the *Temple Inn*.

On a foggy night I set off at 5.30pm for the 7.00pm meeting in Ryhill village school. It was a whole new world for me and the discussion and arguments were difficult to understand, but reporters are expected to understand everything in life and in later years I realised that too much was expected from junior reporters, some aged only seventeen or so.

My story from that night was a complaint about the grave digger who had dug a grave too small. The coffin had to be removed and the family sent to wait in the chapel while the grave was enlarged. The headline on the *Chronicle* story was 'Grave Issue'.

Parish councils provided excellent stories because the councillors were in touch with the community. As they walked the streets they would make note of problems and raise the matter at the next meeting.

South Hiendley had its own council room and I was there on 5 November when local lads threw fireworks into the room. The story about attempts to 'Blow up the local parliament' made good reading... 'Guy Fawkes visited Hiendley' was also a good news line.

For nearly twenty years I covered the work of Royston Urban Council and it was there that I met George Henry Cooke, founder of the local Labour Party, treasurer of the New Monckton branch of

Cllr George Cooke the famous pigeon flyer.

the National Union of Mineworkers, president of the Social Club and a pigeon flyer.

George lived in a small cottage in Cross Lane. He had a moustache and always proudly displayed across his waistcoat his pigeon flyer's medals. He loved snuff, using it frequently in the council chamber, which was initially in a cottage in High Street and later at The Grove, the house where famous cricketer Norman Yardley was born. His snuff habit resulted in a spittoon being placed near his chair. At times George would sit throughout a meeting in his raincoat and flat cap and rarely agreed with his political colleagues. In fact, in November 1954, he caused the monthly meeting to be closed abruptly for the first time since the council's inauguration in 1896.

The trouble started when the council was considering Housing Committee minutes. George, a councillor for over thirty years, got involved in cross-talk with the chairman, Herbert Griffiths, alleging that he had been given the wrong minutes. When the chairman told him the minutes were the same as those any other member had, Cllr Cooke accused him of being a 'religious liar'. Cllr Griffiths rose to his feet and asked Cllr Cooke to withdraw the remark, adding 'If you don't, there will be no meeting tonight.' Cllr Cooke replied: 'That will suit me fine. I'm not withdrawing. You are a liar.'

Lawrence William Jackson, the local Salvation Army's Corps Sergeant Major, said Cllr Cooke always made such accusations in front of the Press. He told him: 'We have had to listen to you when you have been speaking nonsense.' Then Cllr Griffiths said:

Cllr Herbert Griffiths

'I am not going to have such talk. It has gone on for years and every chairman before me has been called names by Cllr Cooke. I vowed when I took office that I would take drastic measures if ever he did the same thing to me. I am not going to have it and I am going to close the meeting.'

The deputy clerk, Harry Benn, then appealed for reason 'because there is a lot of important business'. Cllr Cooke interrupted all the speakers until Cllr Jackson told him he should be ashamed of himself, to which Cllr Cooke replied: 'I have ridiculed no-one and I am not ashamed of myself.'

Julia Westwood, who was often the target of Cllr Cooke's verbal outbursts, then added her appeal for calm. In the end the meeting was closed – after just five minutes. Cllr Cooke was chairman of the Health Committee and made repeated requests for a 'ladies' urinal' in Midland Road. He always topped the poll at election times, but sadly three days after the outburst he was expelled by the local Labour Party of which he had been a founder member.

For years I had been writing about a proposed community hall for Royston and a public subscription fund had been opened. It was to be a memorial hall for those who had died in the two World Wars. Plans were finalised and the Urban Council and the Coal Industry Social Welfare Organisation decided to find the majority of the finance. The stipulation from CISWO was that it should be built of bricks made by the National Coal Board. The contract was given to Royston Builders Limited and it was the first major contract undertaken by Harold Fearn, after the death of the founder, his father Walter. Work started at a site at The Grove in 1963 and councillors visited a Midlands brickyard to select a suitable type of brick. An order was placed by the council but when they arrived at the site Cllr George Smith said they were not the chosen colour. Nevertheless building started and 4,000 bricks were laid. The progress was monitored by architects and councillors until it was decided the bricks were indeed the wrong colour. A visit was made to a Newcastle brickyard and another colour of brick chosen. When they arrived, so did a BBC Television crew who wanted an item about how a 'Council dropped a brick'. Someone had, because although the building was by then more than four feet high – with concrete in the cavities – it had to be demolished and rebuilt with Mitford grey bricks. As the camera recorded, a pigeon landed on the bricks, to which Harold Fearn responded: 'It's chaotic, but it's not my pigeon, it's the council's.' The hall cost nearly £20,000 and the Coal Board also reimbursed the council with the £2,000 cost of knocking down and rebuilding the hall.

Under its clerk of works, Joe Arblaster, it was a progressive council and one of the first to take the drudgery out of the council house kitchen. Through a firm called Moores at Wetherby, it refurbished all the kitchens with new sinks and units. Council tenants were able to see the new kitchens on display in the council offices. They also enjoyed a drink, Watney's Best Bitter, coming from a kitchen tap. The story of that idea got me an end-piece on that night's ITN *News at Ten*.

Councillor George Smith, who threatened to sit in the trees, with left, Ada Bulmer, his wife Mary and Freda.

The council offices were well situated and surrounded by trees. When a plan for widening adjoining Station Road was put forward it meant several of the trees would have to be chopped down. Cllr George Smith, a keen environmentalist in those days, threatened to take up residence in the trees to protest. His battle was successful and the reason Station Road has two widths along its stretch even today, from the Police Station to beyond the Council Offices is due to George's protest.

One meeting heard that local lad Eddie Holliday, who played outside-left for Middlesbrough, had been chosen to play for England. It was decided to send him a congratulatory telegram, the cost of which would have to come from the chairman's allowance. Instead, chairman Lawrence Jackson passed his hat around the table to collect money for the cost of the telegram. In 1960, Eddie played for England against Wales, Ireland and Sweden.

Labour councillors controlled all the local councils and fine Independent councillors like Royston's Tommy Dyer and Cudworth's Horace Richards, never stood a chance with their ideas, even if they were the best. They were always denied chairmanships of the councils, but eventually were honoured when a younger breed of Labour councillor came on the scene.

Bernard Bateman was the power behind Cudworth Urban Council and Independents elected to that authority got under his skin. On one occasion he called two of them by a very rude name. They were stunned and asked for an apology at the next meeting!

Some councillors complained that Cllr Bateman always had his comments reported, perhaps that was because he knew what he was talking about. He made news, but sadly got his 'h's' in the wrong place.

There were times when Eddie Croft's hearing-aid interfered with council business and he was requested to turn down the volume. On one occasion he accompanied local Labour Party member, Charlie Wraith, on an election campaign and Charlie stopped several times because he thought there were problems with his car. It was discovered the crackling sound was coming from Eddie's hearing aid.

When other reporters left the paper, I was asked to cover Grimethorpe council and education committee meetings. The welcome I received in the village was very friendly, especially when John Brailsford was clerk. The business at my first meeting, however, had members puzzled. It was a request from the grave digger for an electric kettle. They were puzzled because the cemetery did not have a power supply.

There was also the occasion when a request came from the youth club in the park to permit be-pop sessions in the pavilion. Councillors said they had no idea what such dancing was like and one asked: 'Is it like a quick waltz?' Chairman Herbert Taylor said there was only one way to find out, attend a dance. The council did, on a summer's evening, and were impressed with the teenagers' dancing, although one feared the floor would be damaged. The dancing sessions were approved.

Cllr Taylor

Although flanked by heavy industry, Grimethorpe had its beauty spots and one was The Dell. Councillors were discussing flooding the area to make a lake for recreation purposes. It was suggested that the council get a gondola, to which Harry Ralph replied: 'Why not get two and breed with 'em.' The comical remark lived on for years.

Cllr Taylor was sponsored, like many councillors, by the Yorkshire Miners' Association and a weekly wage was guaranteed even when on council business. A bungalow on Michael's Estate, owned by the council clerk, was his home and it was said he was quite lenient about rent being paid. There were regular visitors to his home, including local undertaker Harry Walker, who had a good business because his son was a doctor!

One morning he called on Herbert for advice and found a body in a coffin on his hand cart. He said the family of the deceased did not want the body in the house and in those days there were no chapels of rest. He asked him, as council chairman, if he would allow him to keep the body overnight in the welfare hall. But Herbert Taylor told him:

'Ah can't help thee this time and it's fust time ahve known a corpse seek fresh lodgings.'

Harry, in his tall black hat and tail coat, was well known and teenagers would sing this rhyme:

'You may roam about forever, but Harry Walker will nail you in the end.'

Herbert was also called upon for advice about the Sunday opening of the local cinema, because at that time such decisions were only made by a referendum of electors. He said it would need a visit to London – for some reason – for several councillors. This was agreed and they were taken by council taxi to Doncaster railway station for the journey to the capital. When the vote succeeded, they requested the first Sunday night's takings, which were delivered in two satchels, and the family stayed up half the night counting the money.

One Houghton parish councillor was known for his good dress sense. Like most councillors, he fought for a place on the annual conference list and was always successful. He told me he returned to Grimethorpe after every conference with a new coat and hat. During the week he checked out the cloakroom and on the Friday night 'took his pick' and left early!

Hemsworth Rural Council was a dynamic authority ruled by the Henry brothers, Billy of Havercroft and Peter, a Shafton shopkeeper. They were also members of the West Riding County Council and although Billy could not read or write, served the area well. What he said, was done!

But when the council bought the Brierley Hall from Captain Addy, there was an uproar because they wanted to spend several thousand pounds on a carpet. That needed another delegation to London to make a choice and one member said:

'I would have preferred a Persian carpet, then we could have gone to Persia.'

Henry-power was challenged in the chamber by Casto Alonso, a Spanish teacher from Ackworth School. He attacked every move and when Billy Henry tried to keep him quiet, even took a stopwatch into the chamber to make sure he got his allotted time.

School meetings were just as funny and members were often also councillors. Some tried to influence headteachers, especially when non-teaching assistants were introduced to schools, their families were only too ready to take the posts. At one school where a teacher was wanted with music qualifications, the chairman said he would like his daughter to have the job. When asked what special musical qualifications she had, the reply was: 'She can play the recorder and is taking piano lessons.'

The meetings were often complex because of the power of the councillors and the sought-after power of officials. Stan Bristow, a top local journalist who started Mike Parkinson on his rounds, was a great help and a true gentleman of the Press.

When I became chief reporter for the *Chronicle* my council cover turned to Barnsley Borough Council in the majestic Town Hall. But it was no match for the new Hemsworth council chamber with its microphones making a setting as good as the United Nations. Barnsley Council never generated the same humour or top stories.

In 1974 when local government was reorganised, the South Yorkshire County Council was based in Barnsley, and I joined the Press team that each week covered events. Prominent was Enid Hattersley, mother of Labour stalwart Roy, and a young David Blunkett and his guide dog. He was ambitious and is now the government's Education Secretary. Norman West was chairman of the Highway's Committee and he went on to become a European MP. It was a dynamic authority filled with wonderful ideas and it was sad when local government was again reorganised.

Because of my insight into local councils, I have never had any party political interest, although Labour have accused me of being a Tory and the Tories accused me of being Labour. My only political affiliation was the Labour League of Youth at Royston run by Trevor Bell and Jack Hudson, in the Ship Hotel. Councillors do some wonderful work, but politics should not come into matters where the public are concerned.

When Royston Urban Council went out of existence in 1974, councillors presented me with a plaque with the town's coat-of-arms. In 1993, when I retired as editor of the *Chronicle*, Barnsley Metropolitan Council generously gave a civic dinner and leader, Hedley Salt, presented me with a miner's lamp.

Off the Diary

*E*ach day in the news room the diary was marked out for reporters to attend magistrates' court, coroners' inquests, council and education meetings, or other special events.

Reporters were expected to get 'off the diary' stories, those they found through their own initiative and contacts. Some had a flair for this work, others were happy to do what they were asked and nothing more. Exclusives, stories to be first published in the *Chronicle*, could often win a 10s (50p) bonus.

My first 'off diary' was from Bretton Village where retired woodcutter George Walker, who was seventy-seven and a bachelor, declared on his mother Helen's 100th birthday, that a man's best friend was his mother. Helen thought she was 104 because of the figures 1845 on her birth certificate, but checks proved that this was the number of the certificate; born in 1849, she had gone to live at Bretton fifty years earlier when her husband had been made coachman to the Fountains of Birthwaite Hall.

Other special stories included: two successful businessmen with inseparable, identical twin wives who gave up their careers in order to comply with a medical recommendation that their wives should get together again. They were Edith Sutcliffe, wife of Leonard Sutcliffe, of Royston, and Ethel Robinson, wife of Sydney Robinson, of Gainsborough. The families lived together under the same roof for the first nine years of married life after a double wedding, but then went their separate ways. They wrote letters to each other each day and visited once a week. Never happy without each other, they eventually went to run an hotel at Skegness, where their health improved.

Many of my stories were published around the world and one concerned the planting in Royston Welfare Park, in the summer of 1949, of highly-scented flowers by park keeper Selwyn Atack. He had been touched seeing blind people sitting near flowers they could not see, so he planted the scented flowers, white alyssum, mixed stocks and nicotiana, identifying them with Braille labels.

One of the unluckiest people I met was Ernest Elliott of Royston, who worked for forty-three years in the pits. He first went underground at the age of nine, served in the Boer War and then returned to the pits where he suffered five accidents, of which one

Brian Burton as a teenager, gets the guide dog my campaign helped to buy eighteen years earlier.

resulted in a 12-month hospital stay. After ten operations he gave up working and with a £500 grant from New Monckton Colliery started pig breeding. But the pigs died and a few days later his wife died, leaving him with a family of fifteen children. When he was aged seventy he told me:

> *'Misfortune has always dogged my footsteps. Accidents will happen and I have experienced my full share of them.'*

Ex-Corporal Henry Copeland, lived with his daughter in East End Crescent, Royston and, when he was ninety-five years old, told me how he had witnessed the death of the last of the Royal Bonapartes, the Prince Imperial, only son of Napoleon III, the last Emperor of France. He was serving with the Royal Engineers near Itelezi, Zululand in June 1879, when the Zulus charged and killed the Prince as he tried to mount his horse. Harry found the Prince's body stripped of everything but sacred medals given to him by his mother, the Empress Eugenie, when he volunteered for service in South Africa.

Weekly newspapers can help community causes and one of my

first attempts was at Carlton, where it was decided to buy a guide dog for two-year-old Brian Burton. Spring Lane School started the campaign and after the *Chronicle's* publication of an appeal for tinfoil, the school was flooded with sacks of the stuff from all over the country. Money was quickly raised for the dog and put in trust until Brian was old enough to care for, and benefit from, a guide dog. Fifteen years later the Burton family remembered the help I had given and invited me to a Doncaster hospital where Brian was given the dog.

A romance between two blind people ending in marriage, stirred the hearts of residents of South Hiendley. Gertrude Mildred Poole, of South Hiendley, and James Lee, of Bradford, fell in love while on holiday at a Scarborough blind centre, although they had never seen each other. Their courtship lasted four years and at weekends they would visit each other. Their honeymoon was spent in Newcastle after a wedding at Felkirk Church. They said their marriage had brought a new 'light into their darkened lives'. Their greatest thrill they said:

'Was when a friend guided our hands to cut our two-tier wedding cake.'

The 5 February 1955, was special for the small mining community of Woolley Colliery, for it was the wedding day of village heroine Molly Chadwick, who was twenty-one and had no legs. Her friends and neighbours travelled in a special bus to Darton Parish Church where she was married to 22-year-old Leslie Hanson, of Bradford. She was assisted down the aisle by her father, as she walked with her two artificial legs, aided by a walking stick. She stood throughout the twenty minute service.

Born physically handicapped, Molly spent much of her early life in hospital and at the age of eleven had her left leg amputated at the knee and in 1954 she had to have the right leg amputated at the thigh. The couple met at a Leeds hospital and throughout the years Molly was never known to brood or worry about herself, being known to villagers as 'Smiler'.

In August 1952 a Cudworth miner served twenty-eight days in prison for not repaying Public Assistance money he had received twenty-six years earlier. Thomas Sargesson, aged fifty-one at the time, had been paid the money during the miners' stoppage which dragged on after the General Strike in 1926. In 1952 he had an income of 19s (95p) a week - 11s (55p) Army pension and 8s (40p) Public Assistance and he was one of many whom the West Riding

Public Assistance Authority was pressing to wipe off the 26-year-old debts, even to the extent of having defaulters sent to prison. Twice he was summonsed to pay 5s (25p) a month, but he could not manage it. He joined the army, was discharged unfit and was summonsed again. He offered to pay but was taken ill and for six years nothing happened. Then yet another summons for the £10 4s (£10.20) still outstanding arrived and Barnsley Court ordered, if it was not paid, he must go to prison. He was duly taken to Leeds Prison.

Thomas told me:

'When a bailiff came to the door I had ten pence in my pocket. It seems a bit thick to imprison you for not paying money while on Public Assistance.'

Arthur Horner, Secretary of the National Union of Mineworkers, who investigated the case, said:

'It's the craziest thing I've heard of.' The WRPAA said it intended pursuing the defaulters. The story was later published as a splash lead in the 'Sunday People'.

Darton School caretaker Cecil Sunderland bought the 400-year-old Darton Hall, but he finished up with it on his hands. For seventeen years he had been caretaker at Darton Hall Modern School across the road and he had always admired the hall with its ivy-covered walls and spacious interior, just the place for his wife, two sons and a daughter. The school governors insisted that, as caretaker, he must live in the caretaker's house and not the hall fifty yards away. The governors' excuse was:

'We sympathise with Mr Sunderland, but if we let the caretaker's house and he then leaves our employment we would have no house to offer a new caretaker.'

Harry Hull, was a real character and had a scrapyard in Wakefield Road, Barnsley. He received a series of hoax telephone calls and visits to his bungalow in Smithies. He was asked to collect scrap from Wigan and he sent two fourteen-ton lorries the seventy miles, only to be told no one knew anything about the transaction. Returning home, he found a firm unloading five tons of seed potatoes and then following was a procession of vehicles carrying five tons of sand and gravel, eight tons of coal, twelve-inch drain pipes and 7,000 bricks. In fact, £3,000 worth of goods he had not ordered.

The series of hoaxes reached its peak with a knock on his door.

Harry answered and found a man in a dark suit who said he had come to carry out 'Mr Hull's last wishes.' It was a man from Wilf Hyde, undertakers, of Summer Lane, Barnsley, coming to prepare his body for cremation. Mr Hyde said:

> *'We received the request from someone with a husky voice on the telephone. It was quite a shock for Harry.'*

Harry said:

> *'I do not know that I have any enemies, but in this business there are always jealous hearts.'*

Animal stories are always well read and I was asked to call at the Cudworth Hotel to see a dark-haired young lady with a pretty face and trim figure, a pantomime idol and a heavy drinker. I thought I was in for an interesting time until I discovered it was a pony. It was 'Dixie', a New Forest pony with neat legs, glossy coat, bright flirtatious eyes and a thirst for beer greater than the heaviest local drinkers. She was owned by Carl Dane and performed tricks in the concert room, ending by going to the bar and enjoying three pints of beer and a Guinness all from a real glass. Carl was equally famous, for he was the man who struck the gong at the beginning of J. Arthur Rank films, taking over from the famous boxer, Bombardier Billy Wells.

Geoff Richards and myself went into the lion's cage on Shafton Green, the beast being sedated by a bottle of Co-op milk.

Miner Denis Thompson with his wife Mary, at the side of the baby's grave he had dug.

In July 1952 6-year-old Geraldine Gibson, of Mapplewell, sailed with her aunt for Accra on the African Gold Coast, but wept because she had to leave behind her dearest pal, Flash, an Alsatian. For nine months Flash fretted, but then Geraldine flew 4,000 miles home - alone - so they could be reunited.

Another animal call was to neighbouring Shafton, where residents around The Green complained that they could not sleep for a lion's roar. It came from a coach parked on the land by Naomi, a show business personality who was on his way to the Isle of Wight with the performing lion which was kept in a cage in the coach. When Geoff Richards and I went to see what all the noise was about, Naomi invited us into the cage and the lion drank a pint of Co-op milk and was quite friendly. After a few days they went on their way south.

In 1964 I wrote one of the first stories about hole-in-the-heart surgery and the patient was Elizabeth Ann Goose, who lived in Engine Lane, Shafton. Like so many local teenagers, she had to travel to work in the textile mills of West Yorkshire and although she had been treated locally, no one had diagnosed a heart problem. She collapsed on the coach near Halifax and was taken to hospital, where she was told she had a hole in her heart. She had surgery at Killingbeck Hospital, Leeds and on Easter Saturday she was married at Grimethorpe Church and she invited me to the event. She said: 'Your story brought me many friends and much happiness.'

Clergymen were often in the news, at times because of their pompous opinions concerning weddings, baptisms and funerals. In some instances they were correct, because so many people, I found, use the services of churches when they feel like it – four-wheeled Christians. They either go in the pram to be baptised, in a limousine to be married or the hearse to be buried.

During the hot weather of June, miner Dennis Thompson, his eyes blinded by tears, worked stripped to the waist digging a grave for his baby... at a vicar's suggestion. For when he called on the Reverend Tom Boyard-Webster, at Felkirk Church, near South Hiendley, to ask if his only son could be buried in the churchyard, the Vicar told him:

'You can bury your boy here, but you'll have to dig the grave yourself. The grave digger is on holiday.'

He gave the instruction: 'Dig the grave near the wrought iron gates.' Dennis, heartbroken, got a pick and shovel and went the half mile to the churchyard where, after more than three hours' digging, he returned to the Methodist Church for the funeral service. 'I did not have the Vicar conduct the service because I was disgusted,' he said. He took a shovel in the funeral car to fill in the grave after the service, while mourners waited at the gates. The Vicar remarked:

'I can't see anything wrong with Dennis digging the grave. I couldn't get a digger so it seemed the sensible thing to do. I was helping the family to get the funeral over quickly before the Whitsun holiday. I don't regard my actions as un-Christian. He did make a mess digging the grave – it was in the wrong place!'

Dennis added: 'The Vicar only charged me half price - £1 12s 6d (£1.62½ - for burying William because I had dug the grave myself.' Obituaries could be an embarrassment and the correspondents from Darton and Woolley Colliery picked up the story that the oldest man at Woolley Village, John Wood, had died. They both submitted the copy and I was asked to re-write the story. It appeared in the paper, but relatives telephoned to say that, although he was ninety-five, he was still alive. I was asked to go and apologise to John Wood at Pear Tree Farm which was later to become the home of cricketer Geoff Boycott.

His daughter led me to the bedroom where he smiled, I apologised, shook hands with John and was pleased it was all over.

For a period I was freelancing for the *Chronicle*, because of a dispute in March 1950 between the company and the National Union of Journalists. They claimed the paper was employing too many juniors in relation to the seniors. They said the company had to pay more senior rates but they refused, so five youngsters, including me, had to leave. Alan Ridgill (later to become sports editor of the *Daily Mirror*) and Roy Trueman (a future national newspaper manager), were allowed to stay a few months before being called up for National Service. I was on the dole again for months, earning 24s (£1.20) a week, but Ronald Yates, who had become a character like Captain Mainwaring in *Dads' Army*, was upset by the action and eventually offered me a permanent editorial post.

Again off-diary stories started to come my way and one concerned a message to the office for a reporter to go that night to Grimethorpe Working Men's Club because a Lord was to make a visit. Arriving at 9.00pm, I found Screaming Lord Sutch on the stage with a toilet seat around his neck!

While on the subject of toilets, there was the story about Grimethorpe residents complaining when a new toilet block was built opposite the parish church. They had been labelled MEN and WOMEN – they demanded they be named LADIES and GENTLEMEN. The council duly agreed and pride was restored.

The tough miners of New Monckton Colliery suddenly became members of the National Coal Board's most exclusive fishing club, right in their own pit yard. To save the men miles of off-duty travel to fishing spots, the board gave them a half-mile long pool which had

Three wait for a bite at the New Monckton pit lazy lagoon.

been used to put out slag heap fires. The water was tested and then stocked with 800 bream, perch, rudd, roach and carp costing £55. Members paid 15s (75p) a year to fish there. The setting was not attractive. It was surrounded by a slag heap, a coal marshalling yard, a 500ft high 'Blackpool-Tower-like' pit head gear and the pit offices. Dickie Grant said:

'The lads feel at home in their own pit yard. They go home and change out of their pit muck and then go straight back to the pit - to fish.'

The lifestyles of circus folk, gypsies and Romanies have always been a fascination, and one of my first claims on editorial expenses was to cover meeting such people.

Barnsley did attract travelling families, but not many genuine gypsies. I found a family in Burton Bank and paid them 10s for an interview.

Editor, Ronald Yates called me to his office on the Thursday afternoon when the total editorial expenses for eighteen people, were £12. He crossed my 10s from the form with the remark, 'I'm not paying out money to alien gypsies and where's the receipt?' So that was that... a receipt from a gypsy! But it was too late for him to kill the feature, and it appeared in the

The covered wagon which Malinda Lee used as home in true Romany style.
Relaxing by the camp fire.

following day's paper.

In February 1968, Christopher Thackrah was classed as one of the most courageous men of the time. He had become a domestic science teacher at Grimethorpe Secondary Modern School. When he applied for the post he was, not surprisingly, the only man among the applicants. But the selection committee was impressed with his record at college, where he was the only man among 400 women on the domestic science course. Immediately he had one success, a lad who was too shy to ask to join the class when it had a woman teacher. Christopher was soon getting calls from mothers who wanted to know how to get creases out of the settee covers they had washed and how could they brighten up sausage, egg and chips for their husbands.

Requests for help came in to the *Chronicle* offices every week and in 1969 Dr Gerald Sandler, consultant physician and director of the coronary care unit at St Helen's Hospital, asked if I could help him to raise money for a coronary care ambulance for Barnsley which would cost about £5,000. He had seen such an ambulance in Belfast and thought it could save twenty-five lives a year in Barnsley. I attended his lectures and although going back nearly thirty years, I can remember the main cause of heart disease being stressed – smoking. Appeals were made and *Chronicle* readers were quick to respond, raising nearly all the cash required which enabled the ambulance to be commissioned in January 1970. At that time 250 patients a year were admitted to the four-bed coronary care unit, which was supervised by Sister Fawcett. That campaign formed the basis of the new District General Hospital's coronary care fund-raising policy.

The local hospital always generated stories and letters to the paper and in April 1977, when the second phase of the new District General Hospital was opened three years later than expected at a cost of £20 million, a dispute raged on for several years after a complaint was made about lack of instruments and temperature control in the operating theatres.

As news editor, I always encouraged reporters to spend more time out and about meeting people rather than sitting at the desks making contacts by telephone. On a Wednesday morning, with everyone out of the office, the telephone rang and I was asked to send a reporter to the new 810-bed hospital's operating suite. Being the only one around, I went myself and met a team of surgeons, still in their operating gowns and masks, who explained what they described as a disgraceful situation. They were led by Sharad Mahatme, the ear, nose and throat consultant surgeon. For months the argument went on and at one stage the operating theatres were closed. At the centre of the complaints was how a baby in the theatre for an eye operation had to be wrapped in tinfoil to maintain its body temperature.

The Area Health Authority, naturally, was not happy about the stories and letters and pointed a finger at me for keeping the stories running, believing that consultants were keeping me informed. When I revealed that the tinfoil baby, was Baby Rook, their suspicions grew. But how wrong they were, because I discovered the identity of the baby by a bit of journalistic luck.

One day walking along a hospital corridor I met a young mother whose husband had been a leader in my Scout Group. In her arms was a baby wrapped in a blanket. The baby had had eye surgery and I asked: 'Is that the tinfoil baby?' She said it was and I was able to produce an exclusive story and photograph to which the *Chronicle* never gave the presentation it deserved – it went at the bottom of an inside page rather than as a main front page story. This was later done by the national papers, when they used it two days later.

Letters, highly critical of the hospital, were submitted by readers and every one was checked out. We found some of the letters, although signed, had been sent with addresses of unoccupied houses and fictitious properties.

Andrew Butters looked a gentleman and was a gentleman. He was a shy and private person and never sought publicity about his job as consultant surgeon at Beckett Hospital. When he decided to retire his staff invited me to the hospital to interview him in the operating theatre as he finished his last day's task. I was the only journalist he would trust and allowed me to write his retirement story which he wanted to check before publication. We became great friends and, before he died in June 1994, he made a special request that I write his obituary. Although retired from the paper, I was proud to do that for Andrew and his widow Aileen.

Journalism and news reporting were exciting, but to get full satisfaction from the profession the work means a twenty-four-hour, seven-days-a-week involvement. On my bedside table I kept a note-book and pen beside the telephone because contacts would ring at all hours with news items. For instance, Fred Richardson, secretary of Cudworth Garden Society, would ring every Sunday night at 11.30pm with the day's show results.

Alistair Cooke, once said in his BBC *Letter from America* programme, that a journalist who said he was on holiday had, in fact, retired. A good journalist never loses his nose for news.

Howards' Way

T he Howard brothers became famous in 1986 when Barnsley Council wanted to evict them from their home, Rose Cottage, in Worsbrough Common. Real Barnsley characters, they could often be seen in the town centre. Bill was usually pushing his bike and Gordon strolling in the street chatting to shoppers.

They hit the headlines in the *Chronicle*, national newspapers and television with their determined fight against eviction. They became so famous that a television documentary was made about them. As editor, I thought it was time we had a reporter inside the cottage and called for volunteers. Staff reporter Bill Blow was first to put his name forward 'because I am army trained and know how to get over such obstacles'.

Bill, smart, upright and carrying himself in the style of a soldier, looking very much like 'Foggy' in *Last of the Summer Wine*, was the only volunteer, so he was sent with junior reporter Paul Whitehouse. Once at the cottage, Bill suggested that Paul get through a gap in the fence, which he did.

The nation got behind the brothers, but to no avail. They were eventually evicted to make way for a new housing development, but few knew that the two characters were very much part of Barnsley's social scene. Bill, Gordon and their family owned the 'Howards' Academy of Dancing', once the town's leading ballroom, situated in Jackson's Yard, off Dodworth Road. It had the finest ballroom floor in Yorkshire.

At one time dancers at the Academy had to wear full evening dress, tail coats for the men and silk gloves and long dresses for the ladies.

Billy, the dashing tail-coated dance MC.

Slow...slow...quick...quick...slow, famous instructions from any school of dancing could be heard for decades in the Town End district. Thousands of Barnsley folk have memories of dancing five nights a week the Howards' way and apart

The Blue Lyrics Band from the academy days on the set of This is Your Life *at Yorkshire Television studios, Leeds. Subject was Stan Richards of Emmerdale fame.* **Left to right:** *Arthur Kearsley, Stan Richards, Arthur Bird, Bryan Panks, Jack Richmond, Derek Jones, myself and Dickie Bird, who got in on the act.*

from dancers, most local musicians at one time or other also played at the ballroom.

The bands in the gallery appeared to change as quickly as the tempo. At one time the resident band, the Blue Lyrics, invited me to join them. They were a super bunch of teenagers: Stan Richards (piano), Arthur Kearsley and Jack Richmond (piano accordion), Bryan Panks (guitar), Arthur Bird (drums), Charlie Wyatt (banjo) and me, on trumpet.

As a cub reporter whose apprenticeship did not finish until the age of twenty-four, I explained that my regular attendance could present problems, but they said I could join the band whenever I finished work and get the same 5s a session. When we arrived at the ballroom we would meet Gordon in the pay box and Bill would be MC. We would climb the steps up to the band gallery, where, in the interval, we would get a bottle of 'pop' and packet of crisps from the refreshment room.

The Howard brothers were proud of their dance hall and at holiday times special carnival dances were held. Near midnight Bill would come up to the gallery to pull on cords that gave the dancers their 'snowfall' effect. A wire-mesh trough ran the length of the hall and was filled with pieces of paper. It was mostly waste newspaper and it was not unusual to have falling from the roof-mounted trough the remains of the sporting edition. As we played 'White Christmas' and the *Savoy* Christmas Medley, bits from the *Sporting Pink* and Sheffield *Green 'Un* would fall to the ballroom floor, but the dancers never seemed to notice. When things got hot, Bill would take off his black dinner-jacket. It was then that we noticed that he often wore his dress shirt back to front, with the buttons down the back, apparently to get double use between washes. Once we got the sack because they found a cheaper band. We were getting paid less than £4 a night, five nights a week. We met with Bill and Gordon in a nearby public house, where Gordon blamed Bill and Bill blamed Gordon. We never discovered by how much we had been undercut. On the following Monday the brothers would not let us in the ballroom because they feared we would fight the new band, but by the interval we were allowed in. Some time later we returned as the resident band. It was like a summer season at Blackpool.

So many were taught how to dance at the Academy and many people living in the vicinity enjoyed the music. Some locals even claimed that when the band played 'God Save the King' at midnight,

Rose Cottage, which Barnsley Council wanted to demolish.

Billy and Gordon on the
doorstep of the home
they loved.

Left: *Looking sad by the
fireside with their many
pets.*

A setting from the Victorian era, but for the Howard brothers there was no place like home.

Gordon demonstrates that an Englishman's home is his castle.

They warned they would take every measure to protect their home, even by using a rifle.

Protesters supporting the brothers outside Barnsley Town Hall.

they got out of bed and stood to attention.

Whenever Stan Richards and I meet, we cannot stop laughing about our days at 'The Gym', that was the ballroom's nickname. Stan, is a genuine Barnsley personality. We recall how each year we would negotiate a new contract with the Howard brothers and their mother at Rose Cottage. We would not sit in the house, but in the greenhouse with the old lady, Bill and Gordon.

We had to argue hard for 1s (5p) extra a night. They were real characters and I remember it was the only greenhouse in Barnsley growing grapes. They always tried to get a band for under £4 a night. Nonetheless, to us young lads it was like being the resident band at the *Savoy Hotel*.

The Howard brothers were determined not to be evicted and became media stars overnight, but this story shows that Barnsley Council were not the first people to be refused entry to Rose Cottage!

The Howard family had lived at Rose Cottage in Cope Street, Barnsley, for over a century. Gordon and Billy were born there. Barnsley Council wanted the land as part of the Hornby Street Redevelopment Area. They wanted to build much-needed residential

Both the dog and Billy look afraid.

The stress of the siege shows on Gordon's face as the sun rises on his last day at the cottage.

units, mainly for the elderly, in conjunction with a non profit making housing association. Gordon said he would shoot anyone who tried to get them out of the family home where at one time five boys and seven girls lived. The bachelors shared the quiet backwater with several dogs, cats, geese, hens and pigeons.

Following a forty-minute television documentary entitled 'Whose house is it, anyway?', the nation got behind the brothers and jammed the BBC's switchboards with protest calls.

Sadly, the brothers, who were eventually evicted, never did see the programme about them. Their television set was not attached to the power supply!

People

*I*n the 1950s the *Chronicle's* editor, Ronald Yates, and company chairman, Sir Joseph Hewitt, realised the importance of motoring news and asked me to write a weekly feature. Even in those days the feature occupied a broadsheet page and the paper was the first weekly newspaper in the country to feature motoring editorials - other weeklies and, in fact, regional dailies such as the *Sheffield Telegraph* followed.

I was the first journalist on a provincial weekly to be made a member of the Guild of Motoring Writers – that was forty-three years ago – and it brought invitations to new car launches and to meet top motoring executives.

Meeting people is what journalism is all about, no matter what speciality one adopts. For me, it opened the world, which for a weekly newspaperman was a great privilege.

German car maker BMW was the first to invite me abroad for the launch of the 633 Coupe. The destination was the South of France and the journey was by private jet from Heathrow to Nice. The cars were picked up at Nice airport and after a two-hour drive in the mountains we arrived at Domaine de la Trappe, at Vence, owned by actor Kurt Jurgens. He had played the part of Von Trapp in a version of *Sound of Music*, hence the name.

He spoke about his villa and then left the motoring scribes to rest. I was offered the master bedroom which had a bed that could accommodate ten people – I was lost in the middle. Why BMW Public

Domaine de la Trappe, Vence, France, where I met Kurt Jurgens.

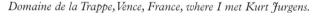

Relations chief Raymond Playfoot offered such luxury to a starter was a surprise, but a bigger surprise was to come during the night.

I was awakened by the patter of bare feet on the tiled floor and as the moon shone through the partly-opened shutters I could see the outline of a naked woman. I felt indulged enough to have such a spacious room and huge bed, but a naked woman walking about... well.

The following morning the mystery was solved. The pilot had brought his wife and they were in the next bedroom – they shared my en-suite facilities. That was the reason for her night-time strolls.

We were mystified by huge brass doors in the floor of the lounge. They were opened to reveal two sunken baths. Kurt Jurgens – like Barnsley folk - enjoyed having a bath in front of the fire.

In 1976 Fiat did not have its own public relations team in the UK and its interests were managed by Woolf, Laing, Christie and Partners, with Alfred Woolf and Tom Northey dealing with journalists. In July of that year they invited members of the Northern Group of Motoring Writers to Turin, the home of Fiat, to tour the factories and see for the first time, the robot-building of cars. The factory was across the road from the Juventus soccer stadium and I stayed at the Hotel Ambasciatori, in the heart of the city. At dinner I sat next to Gianni Agnelli, who at the time was described as 'Europe's most glamorous businessman and the uncrowned King of Italy'. He was head of Fiat and had dealings with prime ministers, the White House, the Pentagon, Moscow and even Colonel Gaddaffi of Libya. Here he was having dinner with a lad from Barnsley and I had difficulty understanding his Italian and equally, I feel, he had problems with my broad Yorkshire accent.

The temperatures during the factory visits had been in the 90s and he asked if I had found it hot. I then made a comment which has never been forgotten by my Northern writing colleagues. 'Aye, an we've had it hot at hooam,' was my reply. He nodded.

The follolwing morning I went to Turin's Cathedral of St John to see the famous shroud - the linen cloth in which Jesus Christ is said to have been wrapped in his tomb. It lies rolled around a velvet staff and wrapped in red silk within a wooden casket with three locks. Occasionally it is put on view, and I was lucky.

A visit to Finland with Ford to test the first anti-lock brakes on the Escort nearly ended in tragedy, for the aeroplane made two attempts to take off from Gatwick, but failed because of instrument trouble. At the third attempt it managed to get airborne, but midway over the North Sea when the altitude meter showed 31,000ft, pressure dropped in the cabin and the aeroplane dropped to 11,000ft. It had to jettison its fuel and head back to Gatwick. Eventually we were put on another aeroplane and arrived at the *Kaivohuone Hotel*, Helsinki, twelve hours late.

It was the hotel used on state visits by kings, queens and presidents and had every facility. Ford personnel knew we were exhausted, so told us to book into the massage room staffed by very attractive blondes. Colleague Keith Ward, of Manchester's *Evening News*, and I found they were fully booked but, as a consolation, we were told we could be treated by big Helga in the leisure suite.

Off we went to the sauna and then were called into the next room by Helga. What we saw was frightening, because she weighed eighteen stone, wore wellingtons and a green rubber apron. There was a bench in the centre and she had a hose pipe in her hand. We were wearing our swimming trunks which she quickly told us to remove and lie on the bench. In turn, we laid on our stomachs and she rubbed lotions into our backs and then for ten minutes scrubbed with a brush. 'Turn over,' she said. We obeyed, but placed our hands over our sensitive parts. She quickly removed our hands. More lotion... more scrubbing. Then we were told to stand against the wall as she demonstrated the purpose of the hose pipe. It was to spray us for three minutes with ice cold water. We were fully rejuvenated and then Helga, who looked sixty, but was in fact only thirty-five years old, said she had come from Russia to find work. She was also a

My first view of the cross above the mini cathedral at the Valley of the Fallen, near Madrid.

The main altar and crucifix made from ebony collected by General Franco.

cleaner at the hotel.

Mazda launched a car in Madrid and we were based at the *Ritz Hotel*, across the road from the famous Prado art gallery. My test route towards the village of Avila, the home of St Theresa, revealed one of the most fantastic views I had seen. It was a giant crucifix set on a hill. It was Santa Cruz del Valle de los Caidos, the Valley of the Fallen and a monument to all who died in the Spanish Civil War. It was in the centre of Spain and was like a lighthouse of faith. At 11.00am each morning priests from the monastery at the rear of the hill celebrate mass and on my visit the sixty priests in their vestments made an impressive sight.

The Abbot came to speak to me and offered me the sacrament, one of the spiritual highlights of my life. The altar before which I stood was beneath the huge exterior crucifix and the little mountain had been excavated to form a mini-cathedral. Behind the altar was the tomb of General Franco who had conceived the idea of the monument and chose the site, along with the ebony for the altar cross which he had cut from nearby woods. The cross-bar of the exterior crucifix is so wide, two cars can pass side by side. The Abbot gave me his blessing and I left the Valley of the Fallen.

Unknown to many, Heathrow Airport has an underground chapel opposite Terminal 2 and if I have hours to wait for a connecting flight, I often go to mass. All denominations use the St George's Chapel and it is a place of peace amidst the turmoil of a hectic airport. With three hours to spare before flying to Morocco, I went to the chapel, arriving as mass was to start. As I knelt, five women in white sat alongside. With their blue-bordered saris I realised they were the Missionaries of Charity.

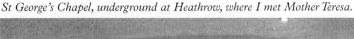

St George's Chapel, underground at Heathrow, where I met Mother Teresa.

Seconds later Mother Teresa of Calcutta, joined them. After the twenty-minute service I went up to her and said how I admired her work for the poor, to which she replied:

Mother Teresa.

'*The greatest poverty in the world is not the lack of food, but the lack of love and friendship. The poverty of the heart is often more difficult to relieve and to defeat. In fact, it is easier to solve poverty than heal a broken heart.*'

She stood holding my hand. She was in a simple cotton habit, a white cotton sari with blue border covering her head, a pair of sandals, a crucifix and a rosary. Her hand was very warm, she said it always was, and added: 'Small things done in great love bring joy and peace.' Mother Teresa and her sisters went on their homeward journey to India and I back to Terminal Two after sharing prayer with a wonderful person. For twenty minutes we had been so far away from the materialistic world.

During a trip to Bolton for a Chrysler Jeep launch local journalist, Derek Grocock, took me to see steeplejack expert Fred Dibner. The front of his house was covered, for some reason, with plastic sheeting, and parked in front was a traction engine and trailer. 'It's grand to meet a Barnsley lad,' said Fred. I asked if he was interested in examining our church steeple, but he said his order book was full. A real lad is Fred.

Prime Minister John Major invited me to a lunch in Leeds and before he arrived six dog owners arrived as though they were preparing for a show. We were asked to leave the room while the dogs went sniffing for bombs. When the all clear was given he had lunch and I found the Prime Minister and his wife Norma extremely friendly. The opinion I gained was that he was the most down-to-earth Conservative leader ever to be at No. 10.

He spoke about the importance of the three 'Rs' and how he planned to put more emphasis on this in education. When Barnsley came up in conversation he asked if I knew Dickie Bird. I said he called at the office nearly every week. He told me: 'He's not very well.' I said I had not heard he was ill and when I got back to the *Chronicle* I asked about his health. A staff member said he was not well, but did not want anyone to know. I thought that was unusual,

World champion ferret-legger Reg Mellor with two of his prize performers.

because I had been told by the Prime Minister that Dickie was ill.

Wandering through the Honeywell allotments in Barnsley I spotted a chap near a garden shed pushing things down his trousers. I watched and he came to the gate. He said he was Reg Mellor and he could keep a ferret down his trousers for hours. At the time I was planning a Barnsley Night to promote the town to northern journalists at the *Ardsley House Hotel.* Already artist Ashley Jackson, Stan Richards (pianist, comedian and great Barnsley character), 'Skinner' Normanton, Michael Parkinson's

Barnsley Night guests.
Left to right: *Ashley Jackson, 'Skinner' Normanton, Freda Parkinson (Mike's mother), Reg Mellor, Anastasia Micklethwaite and Stan Richards.*

soccer hero and young musician Anastasia Micklethwaite, of the National Youth Orchestra had been invited.

Reg said he would do his ferret act at the hotel, but I was afraid they would escape and cause chaos. However, I took the risk and Reg joined the celebrities for dinner during which there was a call for a car owner to move his vehicle. It was Stan Bulmer's, the photographer who had taken Reg to the hotel. The ferrets had been left in two bags, but when Stan opened the door they jumped at him for they had, in fact, escaped in the car.

They were caught and Reg did his party piece. He would place his trouser bottoms inside his socks and put the ferrets down his trousers. It brought him great fame, because he was invited to major events in the UK and spent a month on television shows in Australia, always wearing

Just to let people know he's not fictitious, 'Skinner' Normanton tells me about his new job, as a coal lorry driver.

his Northern Motoring Writers' tie. He was proud of his association with the writers and the letter of thanks I sent him for taking part in events, was framed and hung above his mantelpiece. He also made a video.

During a journey to Leeds along the M1, with his wooden ferret box between his feet, I noticed the lid open and out came the ferrets. I had to operate the hazard warning lights and park on the hard shoulder until they were caught.

Reg held the world record for ferret-legging, more than five hours and to thank me for promoting his hobby, he presented me with 'Syd', a stuffed ferret that had died of pneumonia. Reg died in tragic circumstances, not as a result of his ferret act and inside his coffin he wore his Writers' tie.

Norman Wisdom, the comedian, has always been one of my favourites and when the BBC telephoned to ask if I would take part in a programme with him, it was a great honour. The subject was flat caps. Such headgear was Norman's trademark and the BBC said I

Having a laugh, as usual, with Freda and Norman Wisdom on the Isle of Man.

was a local expert on caps. The broadcast was made with me in the radio studio in the Barnsley Metrodome and Norman from his home in the Isle of Man. The broadcast took 20 minutes and in July 1998, I visited the Isle of Man for the first time for fifty years to write about touring the island. Knowing Norman loved cars, I went to see him and took a cassette of the broadcast. When I called at his country house he was out, but while on the front step a large BMW Eight Series Coupe came down the drive with Norman at the wheel – he had been playing golf. He got out, laughed and tumbled just like he did in his films and welcomed my wife Freda. He invited me into his garage where he kept a 250cc Honda motorcycle which he rides around the island where he is much loved. I told him he was remarkable for an 84-year-old and he said:

'Well, lad, three things happen when you grow old. One is you lose your memory and I can't remember the other two.'

Peter Waring-Smith with his wife, Chia, flat cap and black pudding after travelling from Hong Kong.

Yvonne and Ian Smith with my trophy at Blackpool's new Pembroke Hotel.

A loveable chap is Norman, who was still laughing when we left his home, appropriately called Ballalaugh.

There are characters in journalism as in all walks of life, and a

World-famous driver Sir Stirling Moss hands over my prizes at the Grosvenor Hotel, *Chester, in 1980. Sir Stirling, knighted in 1999, is the greatest motoring icon.*

World motor racing champion Alan Jones presents a writing award at Newcastle.

The man from the moon, Dr Edgar Mitchell. We met at the 1998 Motor Show.

colourful reporter was Trevor Reynolds, the only person I recall who went straight from a weekly newspaper to a national paper. He was a flashy operator for the *Daily Herald* and drove around in an Austin Healey sports car, always with a carnation in his buttonhole and in summer, wore a Panama hat. He would need several pints of beer before he could write, but his operating techniques were unique and successful. To gain one story, he dressed as an Italian airline pilot and stood at the bar of Barnsley's *Royal Hotel*, while on another occasion he arrived on our doorstep one Sunday dressed as a vicar. He was on his way to Gawber church to cover the famous exorcism story. At times he is known to have carried a pair of invalid's crutches in his car - to seek sympathy from anyone who would not give him details. His church visit appeared to give him God's blessing, because he became teetotal and left newspapers to become a Press officer in Lincolnshire.

For two years I was the chairman of the Northern Group of Motoring Writers and one of their biggest events was the annual

Ashley Jackson and myself watch the anonymous artist paint a blind for Monk Bretton Air Scouts during our prison visit.

Mintex test day at Sherburn-in-Elmet. At one event the human star of the show was Peter Waring-Smith, publisher and editor of *Car, Life and Style.* He had flown 8,000 miles from Hong Kong to the test day and at the dinner presentation I handed him a group tie, a piece of black pudding and a traditional Yorkshire flat cap.

A year later at the annual dinner at Blackpool, there was a surprise when I welcomed the deputy mayor to the new *Pembroke Hotel.* The chap who stepped from the civic car was Ian Smith who, along with his wife Yvonne, had lived in Barnsley a few years earlier when he was managing director of *Ardsley House Hotel.* He presented me with the Pirelli Weekly Newspaper Writer of the Year Award, which brought my tally of European, national and Northern writing awards to nine.

The Yorkshire Dales' scene on a cigarette packet painted by a prisoner and handed me as I left.

Other awards were received from Alan Jones, the world motor

racing champion and Stirling Moss, ten times British National
Champion and twice voted Driver of the Year. I was proud to have
dinner with Stirling, a British racing legend and a household name.

Australian Alan Jones travelled all the way from 'down under' to
Newcastle to give the shortest after-dinner speech I can remember.
He simply said: 'It's wonderful to be with you. Have
a nice evening.'

At the 1998 International Motor Show I met
Dr Edgar Mitchell, one of only twelve
humans to walk on the moon. He
launched the new Mitsubishi Space
Wagon and Space Star models and told
me how he served on the back-up crew
for Apollo 10 and 16 and, in 1971, was
module pilot of Apollo 14 lunar
mission making him the sixth man to
walk on the moon. He said that life is
almost certain to exist on other planets
with a supportive environment. He
pointed out that some leading
physicists feel that it is theoretically
possible to travel faster than the speed of
light. His intelligence contacts also told
him that there was a cover up of truth
about UFOs.

There was a man who has to remain
nameless. With local artist Ashley Jackson I
visited Wakefield Prison with permission from
the Home Office. He was teaching art and we
mixed with murderers in a special wing. I took

Heather Mills.

a packet of cigarettes for the prisoners and, as I left, one handed me
the packet. On the inside it said 'thanks' and there was a painting of
a scene from the Yorkshire Dales. He also painted me a roller blind
for the new Monk Bretton Scout Centre. It was of Kettlewell. It bore
no inscription other than: HM Studio, Wakefield.

At Rudding Park, Harrogate, for a SAAB launch, my co-driver was
former swimsuit model Heather Mills, who had lost a leg and her
livelihood when a police motorcycle struck her in 1993. She had an
artificial leg and promoted driving for the disabled and helped land-
mine missions. In early 2000 she became Sir Paul McCartney's
girlfriend.

Places

ore than 680 flights and thirty sailings by ship took me to forty-eight different countries in twenty-five years and I was able to visit some of the most exclusive and fascinating hotels in the world.

France was always a popular venue because of its climate and several times I stayed at *Le Mas D'Artigny*, which is on the summit of a sixteen-acre wooded hill overlooking the entire Riviera, and a short distance from one of my favourite places, Saint-Paul-De-Vence. The hotel has forty-plus suites and twenty sumptuous villas, each with a secluded patio and small private swimming pool. Regular visitors include the President of France.

St-Paul-De-Vence was once a military look-out post, but now is a pretty village with narrow streets where vehicles cannot enter. I was amazed to find that one of my former junior reporters, Janice Gregory, from Great Houghton, lives there, having married a Frenchman.

On the promenade at Nice is the *Le Negresco*, the grandest of the huge seafront hotels. I was welcomed by a porter wearing tights, knickerbockers, cape, plumed hat and white gloves. A wonderful place that has the largest circular carpet in the world. Even in February the place famous for its film festival can provide topless sunbathers.

Monaco (Monte Carlo) is magic, but is being spoiled by huge towers of apartments. It was during a visit here that guide Philippe Borsarelli took me into the mountains and down the road where Princess Grace of Monaco was killed in a car accident. The accident happened at a difficult bend and he told me only one person knew who was driving the car and he had suddenly left the area. There is still a mystery about the accident, but what I was told and reported was later denied when a letter came from the Principality of Monaco's press office.

Paris was one of my regular destinations where my most dramatic night was at the *Palace Hotel*, Versailles, opposite the beautiful palace with its famous hall of mirrors and Marie Antoinette's bedroom. It was dramatic because few of us had a good night's sleep. There was so much banging and sawing in the night. The following morning, as we had breakfast, four men carried out a coffin...

It was during that stay that we went to the Alcazar of Paris show described as 'the best show in the world'. The theatre was down a narrow street lined with drunks and drug-takers, but the Northern motoring writers caused a stir at 2.00am by dancing on the stage with a stuffed ferret on a string.

Each time I visited *Chateau De Chailly* in a pretty village near Dijon, in Burgundy, there was a letter in my room from Olivier de Boynes, the general manager. Jaguar Cars had invited me so many times that the letter always read: 'Welcome back home.' The hotel had been a mediaeval fortress and now is classed as a national monument. One hundred craftsmen worked on its renovation.

Spain was always a popular venue, especially the *Hotel Puente Romano*, near Marbella. Situated on the Mediterranean shore, it has 200 deluxe bedrooms with gold-plated bathroom fittings – even the wash basin taps. The inner courtyard is splendid for summer candlelit dinners.

Not very far away the *Hotel Sotogrande* stands in 400 acres of secluded Andalucian countryside. It overlooks Gibraltar and North Africa and is set between two of the most beautiful golf courses in Europe. When I stayed, I had breakfast with golf commentator Peter Allis and then took a few tips from Tony Jacklin who provided golf clinics.

I have also been privileged to stay at the *Hotel Splendido* at Portofino on the Italian Riviera, where Gina Lollobrigida, Liz Taylor and Sophia Loren slept and the late Princess Diana stole the chef to take to Kensington Palace.

Portofino is small but beautiful and its harbour one of the most colourful in the world. The *Splendido* sits snugly on a terrace cut into the hillside. The bedrooms overlooking the bay are magnificent. Its furnishings throughout are not vulgar. Parking a car is a problem in the area and I dread to think what congestion would be like in summer. A double room with a sea view can cost £460 a night. At night we walked from the hotel to the harbour and had a drink on a floating bar just outside the village's own Armani shop.

Austria can be dull at times, especially near the big cities, yet can also offer much beauty. Visiting Vienna I stayed at the elegant *Hotel Imperial* where official guests of the Austrian Republic also stay. Countless discussions have been held in the luxurious royal suites and reception rooms which have later influenced the course of history. I signed the guest book and on earlier pages were the signatures of our own Queen, Alfred Hitchcock, Rudolf Nureyev, Margot Fontaine, Anwas al-Sadat, Henry Kissinger, Andrej Gromyko, Placido Domingo, Frank Sinatra, footballer Pele and

David Rockefeller.

After having breakfast with racing driver Nikki Lauda – who had an apartment around the corner – I drove through the Vienna Woods and on to Hungary and Bratislava, in the new Republic of Slovakia. I was back in Austria in time for lunch.

Approaching Bratislava I feared traffic congestion, but there was little, with thousands of Trabant cars parked in the streets – the owners could not afford to run them. The people looked poor, the women beautiful and trying to catch up with Western fashions. Churches were just beginning to re-open after Communist domination and the shops had very little to offer customers.

Basket selling in Hungary.

In one street I met famous tennis star Drobny at his sports shop.

The people were very kind and appreciative of every compliment they received. They were very self-conscious that their standards may not compare favourably with those we were used to. For refreshments I went to the *Danube Hotel*, set on the bank of the famous river. There were few residents and the restaurant had only six customers.

My stay was short, but I felt sorry for the people who appeared to be struggling to exist.

In Sweden's Gothenburg, we were taken to a very unusual restaurant. It was not far from the *Park Hotel* where we were staying, but had no waiters. Diners sat at man-made rivers throughout the restaurant with a radio-controlled unit in their hands. The idea was

Crossing the border from Slovakia into Hungary.

With Erik Carlsson at a Swedish test track.

that the diner fetched his own meals from the kitchen by radio-controlled boats. Very novel, but the Japanese visitors were so fascinated by the boats, they never ate anything.

It was during a visit to the Saab factory that I stayed at a country residence, Humdelunda Castle, eighty miles south of Stockholm, used by the company for training. It was a very peaceful place, which was a surprise, because it had been used by Hitler's information chief Hermann Goering in the Second World War. It was filled with artistic riches and we ate in his former dining room.

During my stay I met world famous rally driver Erik Carlsson – he married Stirling Moss' sister Pat – and we drove around the Kinnekulle test circuit. He's the fastest driver I have been in a car with.

A visit to Holland was an annual event for Northern motoring writers over ten years. We visited every part of the country after travelling on North Sea Ferries. Amsterdam is the most fascinating city in Europe, with Anne Frank's house being an emotional place and the Red Light district an enlightening spot. But people who visit the district often miss the Church in the Attic, high above the sex parlours. After climbing many sets of steps, one enters a tiny, complete church which worshippers used when religion was banned. There is an altar, pews and organ.

Morocco is a country full of mystery and on my first visit I had to fly to Casablanca and then travel by small plane over the mountains to Quarzazate. The airstrip did not have any electric lights, so the locals held oil torches alongside the runway. In such an outback, we were met by Glasgow Transport double-deckers which took us to the hotel. It was dark and very hot and we were met by ten tribesmen on white horses, waving flares and swords.

The next day we were off into the wilds, being stopped many times by villagers selling copperware. I bought a copper kettle and discovered the way to check for holes – by holding it towards the sky where light reveals the faults. The tribesmen don't like it.

Lunch stop was at a tiny village with a sign which read: '100 days from Timbuktu'. Children from surrounding villages gathered on the roadside in their best tribal clothing to give a welcome, get attention from our travelling doctor and to collect all the food that was left.

Bryan Longworth and myself walk from the ablutions - sacks of straw - in a village in Morocco watched by dishwashers whose water flowed from the ablutions.

Then there was a daring journey over the snow-capped High Atlas mountains to wonderful Marrakesh with its entertainers, street sellers and even coal merchants. Touts and con men are a real

Children from a village in Morocco flock to greet us.

Locals seem to rest all day in Aswan.

problem and I never trused the official guides.

For a second time I was invited to Morocco, to the Palais Salam at Taroudant, but the night before I was to leave I received a call to say the visit was off. King Hassan had decided to go on holiday to the same place with his staff, so he took over the airstrip and the Palais. Later, however came another invitation and I found the 'hotel', a former palace, a delightful place except for very early morning

Doing a 'Bob Geldof' by feeding the children of Egypt.

Preparing to ride my horse down the canyon to Petra.

loudspeaker Muezzins calling the faithful to prayer.

During a driving test in Morocco I experienced one of my worst nightmares. On a desert-type road, day suddenly turned to night at around 11.00am. It was due to a plague of locusts who had eaten all the available vegetation and formed a huge cloud that covered miles.

The pale green locusts covered the windscreen and car and Bryan Longworth and myself had to battle to keep on the road. When we eventually reached a village the red car we started out with was pale green and water from a stream had to be used to remove the dead locusts.

A church carved from the red rock at Petra.

Mention Egypt and immediately most people will say it is a country they would love to visit. I have toured every part except Cairo and I found it is not a country with lavish landscapes, but has a natural beauty where people blend in with the simple surroundings. When I opened my curtains on the Nile cruiser *Ritz* on the first morning, the scene was the same as I had seen in an illustrated

Bible – it had never changed.

One's first sight of the people and landscape reflects what ancient texts tell us – we can still see them today with our own eyes. From Aswan I drove to Luxor, the spiritual and political centre of Egypt and during the 170-mile journey I saw only three petrol stations. Travelling in Egypt one has to cope with carts pulled by animals, or even people because once they start they will not stop.

Then I went from Aswan to Abu Simbel on the banks of Lake Nasser and into the Temple of Rameses which would have been lost when the lake was flooded. The temple had been cut into 1,000 stone blocks, some weighing 30 tonnes, and lifted from the valley and onto the banks – the task took five years. During my 200-mile journey I met only six other cars and a camel train with 500 camels on its way from the Sudan to Aswan.

My next visit to the country was to Taba near the border with Israel and our aeroplane landed on a military airfield where the pilot had to take great care not to enter Israeli air space. Then it was through the Sinai desert, a great wilderness where the Bedouin nomads roam the arid land of the peninsula. On visits to third world countries I have seen countless folk begging for money and food, but in the Sinai it was children wanting water.

Two years later I was back at Taba, staying on a converted ferry which took me across the Gulf of Aquaba to Jordan, where I made a special journey to Petra.

Petra is called the 'rose red city' and is situated in the south of Jordan. Hidden away amidst the folds of spectacular hills, the site was lost to Europeans until 1812 when it was rediscovered by a Swiss explorer. I entered the once secret narrow gorge on horseback and after twenty minutes was faced with a city carved out of the rock – houses and even tombs. A street of houses had been gouged away from the rock and there is an auditorium that could accommodate 7,000 people. A nomadic group of Arabs settled in Petra which is yet another wonder of the world.

Jordan appeared a modern country, but Egypt is a place where water, sugar cane, a donkey – for the rich a camel – are the main factors of life.

After the Middle East, it was a quick dash to Switzerland and the *Beau-Rivage Palace*, Lausanne, where I was invited by Jean Denton, head of public relations for Rover and now Baroness Denton of Wakefield. It was a classical hotel, again used by monarchs and heads of state, set on the shore of Lake Geneva.

Then back to the South of France to meet Renault's famous pair,

Nicole and Papa, at the *Hotel Les Roches* at Le Lavandou. Clinging to the cliff face it offered everything but a warm bedroom.

I was once included in a party of nine other motoring writers from the UK, all from national newspapers and magazines, and we had been invited by Mitsubishi Motor Corporation of Japan to see their part of the world and tour the Japanese motor industry which was at its peak. I was the only weekly newspaper writer to be chosen, I believe, because I had just won a European motoring award.

We discussed the programme ahead and it was during this period we were told about the hijack of an Al Italia jet with 259 passengers at our destination airport, Bangkok. After various delays and fears that we might be diverted, it eventually took us nearly twenty hours before landing at Don Muang Airport in Bangkok, moving slowly past the hijacked airliner. The sky pirate was standing in the aeroplane's

The Sri Lankan hijacker walks down the steps of the jumbo jet after a two-day drama.

entrance with his arms waving in the air, trying to negotiate terms with the police, who had surrounded the aircraft.

Once out of our jet, the atmosphere was like standing over a gas oven when the door was ajar. It was Bangkok... it was very hot... it was just five degrees from the equator.

Near the airport, scaffolding had been erected by the Thai Television Company to record the hijack. They could not get their cameras near the tarmac so they built a tower on the road to film the incident.Because there had been so many hijacks at Bangkok, they decided to leave the tower erected – for next time!

After touring around Bangkok and other parts of Thailand we moved on to Hong Kong where I was determined to purchase some

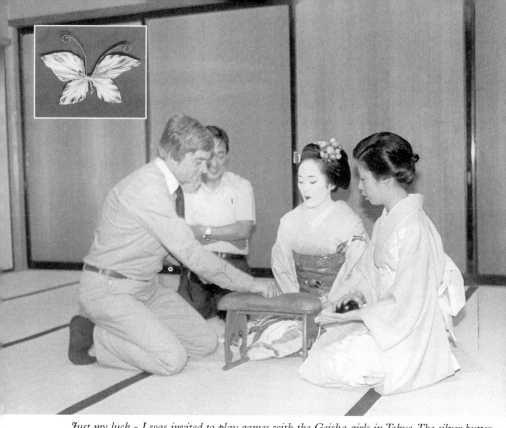

Just my luck - I was invited to play games with the Geisha girls in Tokyo. The silver butterfly, (inset) was made by the Geisha to say 'sorry' for her neglect.

Seated third from the right, front row, with journalists on the world tour, this time Japan.

cheap electrical goods. I bartered for an hour for a mini-pocket recorder and a camera telephoto lens.

I bought the recorder for £34 and the lens for £54 after the shopkeeper had turned white at the ridiculous prices I was prepared to pay. When I left the shop I even looked back through the window to see if he was smiling about the deal – he wasn't.

When I returned to Barnsley, the recorder was £34.95 in Currys and the lens £47 in Comet. I had been done!

One learns by experience and my advice to anyone visiting Hong Kong is: decide what you want to buy and check prices in Britain before you go.

Eventually we arrived in Japan. It is one of the cleanest countries in the world where people believe in beauty and simplicity. It is rare to see a dirty car, tram, truck or graffiti.

The crime rate is low and they are strict on the issue of licences.

For instance, a person wanting a licence for a firearm must first of all go to a hospital to see whether he is of sufficiently sound mind to have such a gun. If he gets an 'all clear' certificate, he then gets the licence.

The people are so kind and love a good laugh. Punctuality and politeness are found everywhere. One also quickly becomes accustomed to the Japanese traditional greeting – the bow.

The children always look bouncy and happy and always look smart. It is rare to see a school party without a school uniform – including hat.

Uniforms seem to form an important part of life in the country and it is not unusual to find traffic controllers, security officers and even car park attendants who could be mistaken for Army Generals. Family links seem very strong and families take great joy from a family walk or shopping expedition. At one time the average family had seven to eight children 'because they were poor and had nothing else to do'. Then the average became two 'because television has helped to limit the birth rate'.

They do have problems with speech, especially pronouncing 'R'. That is why Friday becomes 'flyday'.

To the western world, a Geisha girl is a mystery. The Geisha originated by attending parties held in feudal mansions. Her duties were only to help serve food and drinks and to entertain with songs and dances. Today her duties have not changed. Many believe they are found in bath houses and massage parlours. That is not so, although 'imitations' may be found in such places.

The high-class Geisha is expensive entertainment and those I met earned

£100 an hour. They claimed travelling time, transport costs and tips.

I approached my first encounter with a Geisha rather nervously. The invitation came to attend a 'Sukiyaki' dinner – a traditional Japanese meal – at the Kyo Yamato Restaurant a few miles from the centre of Kyoto. Entertainment, I was told, would be by Geisha and Make girls. After walking through a beautiful landscaped garden with lots of greenery, but no flowers, the Geisha was waiting.

The entrance to the restaurant was dimly lit and there she was kneeling near the threshold, small with a china-like face. She was wearing a beautiful kimono. She bowed, I bowed and then I removed my shoes which were put neatly on a side step. I was asked not to walk on the threshold because, in Japan, to do this is like walking on the forehead of the head of the house or property.

It is just another custom, like leaving one's footwear on the step. The reason is that in the country the majority of people sleep on the floor mat and it would be unfair to walk over their bed with outside footwear.

My guide commented:

'In your country you would not got to a house and walk over the tenant's bed.' I agreed.

The restaurant, like the majority of houses, had a minimal amount of

Girls of Bangkok on their way to the floating market. My hotel, The Oriental, *is in the background.*

furniture. The dining area had only small tables and 'legless' chairs. The tables were only eighteen inches high and chairs had slides instead of legs. The procedure is to sit on the chair and slide under the table.

The Geisha brought warm sake to drink and then various dishes, including the dreaded raw fish. I had been warned about this Japanese delicacy but I found the various types of uncooked fish – tuna looks like raw beef – enjoyable. With chopsticks, the fish is dipped in Soya sauce and other sauces and down it goes.

There was meat cooked at the table on a small oriental stove, but inside was a container of calor gas.

I was nearly chopstick-fed by the Geisha, who knelt alongside throughout the meal. The food was good, but I got leg cramp due to sitting so long in such an unusual situation.

The Geisha, through tradition, is trained to please any man. Her bag of tricks is to make even the most miserable individual forget his worries. So I forgot the cramp!

She then sang and danced but by 9.30pm it was all over. In Japan they believe in retiring early.

My next association with this most famous tradition of the East was at the Hannya-en Restaurant in Tokyo. It was a villa formerly owned by Prince Shimazu.

It is a place of historical significance with a stone monument on which poems describing the scenic beauty around the place are inscribed. They were composed 150 years ago.

I was able to sip lotus flower tea in a garden that has no equal in post war Tokyo as far as time-honoured establishments of typical Japanese styles are concerned.

The room used for dinner had also had as visitors Princess Margaret, President Nixon, Henry Kissinger, Marlon Brando and Yul Brynner. My Geisha hostess told me: 'People from every country in the world have visited here since 1945.'

My Geisha on this occasion appeared more joyful – I think she drank more sake than I did. The food came in small dishes and again was enjoyable, if not filling.

When she turned away, my chopsticks selected raw horseradish by mistake, with the result that within minutes I had hiccups. It was embarrassing as my spasmodic hiccups could be heard around the room and no amount of sips of water, slaps on the back and 'shocks' eased the situation.

The Geisha was so upset by her apparent neglect, that she handed me a large silver butterfly as I left the restaurant. It had been made in a few minutes from the lining of a cigarette packet. It was a souvenir, along with my song sheet, of a memorable night. The visits meant I had flown 18,000 miles around the world in twelve days.

The shadow of James Bond followed me around after staying at the New Otani in Tokyo where his film *On His Majesty's Service* was made. It was at Stoke Poges where Bond defeated Goldfinger on the 18th green in 1964. The clubhouse, course and hotel were the backdrop of the film.

Ahead of me on the fairways was actor Hugh Grant, of *Four Weddings and a Funeral* fame, and great golf lover, Terry Wogan.

James Bond also beat me to the dramatic shores of Costa Smeralda in Sardinia, where I played golf on one of the most exciting courses I have visited. I was based at the *Hotel Cala Di Volpe*. He was there to make the film *You Only Live Twice*.

My visit was also dramatic and needed Bond tactics to escape. That part of Sardinia was, at the time, notorious for kidnappings, especially the Shields family.

Out with colleague Keith Ward – who was driving – we were ambushed by the police and the Volkswagen Polo surrounded by armed men. We were told to get out of the car and Keith was asked to produce his driving licence. He only had swimming trunks and bathing robe, the licence being back at the hotel.

That really started things, and he was asked to stand with arms across the bonnet while under the eye of an armed policeman. I said I would return to the hotel for the licence so waved down a car which kindly took me there. The German organisers were annoyed and went back with me, but Keith was still being guarded when we returned and only allowed to move when the licence was produced and a fine equal to £10 paid to a chap with a cash till in the back of a van. The whole scene was dramatic and I set myself up to take a photograph, but stopped when a gun was pushed into my ribs. I had my licence, but was not driving, and it was a reminder that in Italy one must not only have a driving licence, but it must be carried at all times.

The UK also has classical hotels and *Lucknam Park* at Colerne, near Bath, was used by Rover and Citroen. It was also used for the wedding reception for Princess Diana's stepmother when she married a French Count. I understand she had all the rose beds changed to a colour to match her wedding dress.

The *Imperial Hotel*, Torquay, was, for a while, a popular car launch base and on one visit former Prime Minister, Edward Heath, was recuperating there and in residence was garden expert Percy Thrower. He was running a three-day garden club and in the evening his members invited us to their private dance.

Percy looked very smart in his dinner jacket and black tie, but was very bad on his legs, in fact, his knees were permanently bent. One guest said it was because over the years he had 'spent so much time in the potting shed'.

Writer George Exley was, at the time, secretary of the Scarborough Lifeboat and wherever he went carried his emergency bleep and a big bunch of keys on his belt.

While during the veleta, the band was playing 'I'm forever blowing bubbles', his bleeper sounded – it had picked up signals from Torbay rather than the North Sea.

Another scribe, Bryan Longworth, moved swiftly over the ballroom floor to dance with an attractive gardener, but was beaten by Percy. He had to dance with her mother, who had arthritis and said: 'Thanks young man, I have not had a dance for thirty years.' Peter Ward, who stands five foot two danced with the six-foot tall blonde singer.

Great Fosters country hotel, just seven miles from Heathrow, is another country classic and was featured in the film *A Night to Remember* on the sinking of the *Titanic*. Noel Coward gave it a line in one of his plays. A secret passage through the bottom of a bedroom cupboard was used by Charlie Chaplin to say 'goodnight' to his children.

Cliveden, at Taplow, Berkshire, was the home of the Astor family for five generations. It was also the scene of a scandal that rocked our nation. It was there, on the leafy banks of the Thames, in the summers of the early 1960s, that osteopath Dr Stephen Ward came at weekends with Christine Keeler, Mandy Rice-Davis and the Russian naval attache Yevgeny Ivanov. Into this Cliveden world strayed John Profumo, Secretary of State for War, who took an interest in the 19-year-old Miss Keeler after seeing her topless behind the walls of the swimming pool. Profumo denied it but eventually the Macmillan government was brought down by the ensuing revelations.

At Cliveden, with Renault, I was pampered. The number of staff equalled the number of guests. I swam in the pool where Christine frollicked, sipped Earl Grey tea in my room, but when I got back to Barnsley realised I had left my swimming trunks drying on the room radiator. Who would care at Cliveden? A cottage for a week costs £6,000 so what value is a pair of trunks?

British Pride

There were times during my travels around the world when I was really proud to be British. One such occasion was 17 August 1983, when I flew on Concorde on its first-ever visit to Germany.

Volkswagen launched its new Golf in Munich and flew nearly 100 motoring writers to the city. The popular daily papers at the time said when Barry Manilow arrived on Concorde at Heathrow for his Blenheim Palace concert, he was greeted by 100 fans. When I landed in Munich, 60,000 people were waiting to greet what must be Britain's greastest ambassador.

On our approach to the airport, the fields were filled with spectators and parked cars. The runway had been lined with special grandstands borrowed from the Olympic Stadium. The airport had been brought to a standstill. Once official greetings had been exchanged, the aeroplane was surrounded by television crews and a miniature German beer festival. On a scorching hot day everyone drank to the fortunes of Britain's Concorde. People who have never been near an airport are fascinated by Concorde and a trip on the aeroplane must come very near top of the list of things 'I would most like to do'. At that time the single fare was £1,200.

Concorde is an international express and has established beyond question its unique contribution to the business world, where time, quite simply, is money. But for all its practicality, the fascination of the big bird remains. How else could one travel from New York's Kennedy Airport to Heathrow in two hours, 59 minutes and 14 seconds which Concorde achieved in January 1980? Apart from its wing span, the aeroplane is not large and the interior no larger than the old Viscount aeroplanes. Surprisingly, I found adequate leg room for my trip to Germany which, due to flying supersonic, first went out over the Atlantic. On take-off, the climb is steeper than on the average aircraft and Concorde uses fuel at the rate of 83 tons an hour. Only by watching the digital machmeter at the front of the cabin does one realise supersonic speed is being reached. A 'nudge in the back' is felt as the engine reheats are brought in to accelerate towards Mach 1, not unlike the sensation of an automatic car changing gear. It is exciting when one

*Celebrating under the nose of Concorde, myself, Ken Yeadon (*Yorkshire Evening Post*) and Bryan Longworth (*South Yorkshire Times*).*

reaches Mach 1, the speed of sound. At typical Concorde cruising altitudes this comes at around 670mph with Mach 1.5 at 1,000 mph. We reached Mach 2, twice the speed of sound at a height of 55,000ft and a speed of more than 1,340 mph. It was then the most thrilling experience of my life was recorded. The sky became darker. The familiar blue of the sky is caused by the scattering effect of the earth's atmosphere on the light from the sun. With altitude, the atmosphere becomes thinner, so the scattering is lessened. Hence, astronauts observe a 'black sky' in space. From Concorde's cruising height, I could see clearly the curvature of the earth. Proving the fact that the earth really is ROUND.

Concorde looks like a giant bird and many people ask why it has a 'droop nose'. The long aerodynamic shape of the nose has to be altered to allow greater visibility to the two pilots on take-off and landing. There is also a flight engineer. On take-off the next day from Munich, the large crowd gathered again and we had problems reaching the airport due to the traffic congestion. The pilot signalled farewell after this historic aviation event by dipping the nose to the spectators. The only inconvenience about the aeroplane was the toilets. They were so small they would not have been out of place in an infants' school! The champagne was good, the meal average, but the little salt and pepper pots made special with Concorde symbols by Doulton, are a collector's item. British Airways told me that to book the aeroplane for a day from London to Paris would cost £38,000 and was earning £9 million a year. It cost the taxpayer £1 billion to develop. When the Germans gave it such a wonderful reception and stopped the traffic for half a day, it made one proud to be British.

There was the sad incident on 26 July 2000 when a French Concorde crashed near Charles de Gaulle airport. I hope it wasn't a way for a dream to end!

Not all air travel is luxurious for motoring writers and at times it can be odd and even dangerous. On one occasion a German manufacturer sent an invitation to test a car at Birmingham and offered a private flight from Leeds-Bradford Airport. Four writers accepted the invitation, but on arrival there were just two - Ken Yeadon and myself. We waited at a private hangar looking for the aeroplane and pilots. Eventually, one arrived and said he would take us. 'But where is the aeroplane?' we asked. He said it was in the corner and would we help push it out. Ken and myself looked amazed for it was the first time we had been asked to do ground duties. When the aeroplane was out of the hangar we were then asked to push it to the fuel pump. 'Good job I remembered' said the pilot.

The Burning Bush

One of the greatest Biblical incidents was God speaking to Moses from a burning bush in the Sinai desert and today, reputedly, the 'bush' still grows.

The incident, recalled in the Bible in Exodus, Chapter 3, forms one of the great chapters in scripture and, as people who read the Bible are aware, although it appeared to be burning, the 'bush' was never destroyed. It still grows in one of the most isolated parts of the world, at St Catherine's Monastery at the foot of Mount Sinai, where God handed Moses the Ten Commandments.

During my visit to the Sinai Peninsular in March 1993, testing the new Peugeot 306, I was able to visit the monastery where divine services have been held for 2,000 years and where today it is the home of monks of the Greek Orthodox Church.

Earlier I had arrived by air at the isolated air strip at Taba. Taba is on the Israeli border and next day we set off on a test route of 150 miles. At lunchtime we looked through a gap in the mountains and could see the monastery nestling in the valley. It is situated 500 miles from Cairo and although pilgrims visit the monastery, it can take five hours by coach.

The monastery is home to thirty monks although it can accommodate more than fifty. Some pilgrims decided to stay and one, now a monk, was my guide. He came originally from Devon.

The main church contains sacramental lamps, given mainly by the Russian Orthodox Church, and is filled with icons of great historical significance which have been donated by churches throughout the world. In the centre of the Church is the Archbishop's throne and set in the roof are symbols of the Moon and Sun. At Easter only the Sun symbol is opened and the sun's rays shine down on the Archbishop's

The Burning Bush surrounded by a protected wall.

The monastery gardens with Mount Sinai in the background.
The Russian icons inside St George's Church.

throne.

The monks are helped in their tasks by local Bedouin tribes although during more than 300 miles of travel I met only thirty Bedouins and their camels.

The monastery contains a very important Biblical library in the world, second only to the Vatican and I saw some original New Testament manuscripts, but not Old Testament, which are said to have been there at one time.

They were taken away by a German in 1846 and given to the Tsar of Russia to pay off his debts. Today they are in the possession of the British Library who paid the Soviet Government £100,000 in 1934, so they could be preserved in this country.

They were bought through public subscriptions and a government grant and attracted hordes of visitors to the British Museum when they were first displayed there, and where the monks of St Catherine's still think they rest.

The New Testament manuscript was tampered with centuries ago, but laser equipment now used in outer space has brought about the original writings.

There is a metal casket presented by a Russian princess which contains the last remains of St Catherine, a skull and arm. Other parts were taken by the Crusaders and distributed in various parts of the world. Also in the monastery grounds is the charnel house where the skulls of deceased monks are kept. When people die in the Sinai, they are buried under stones and later removed. In the monastery, they are preserved – just like the remains of St Catherine which are revealed on special feast days.

There is a touch of twentieth century irony in this, one of the most holy places on earth. Behind the main altar of the Church is a tiny chapel containing the roots of the Burning Bush. Because the ground is deemed to be holy, visitors are required to remove their shoes and very few are allowed to see the altar of the Burning Bush, but I was privileged to be invited. The tiny chapel is tiled in blue and white ceramics from Damascus. Services are held in the chapel each Saturday.

The Bush originally grew outside the Church, but the monks decided to make it into a shrine and when this was built, there was no roof to allow the sun and rain to get to the Bush. Later it became so big that it extended to the exterior of the Church where it is now protected by a stone wall. Although people have taken cuttings none has succeeded in growing the Bush, even in other parts of the Sinai. In the chapel there is a modern fire sprinkler system – no doubt to

Tom Horsfield and myself check the height of the bush after five months at his Silkstone nursery. **Inset:** *The tiny cutting taken at the monastery.*

make sure it does not burn again. Or is it just to preserve one of the most historic Biblical stories of all time?

Later, while refreshments were being taken to the library, I dashed back to the Bush and took a cutting while no one was watching. I also filled a bottle with water from the well where Moses met his wife. After motoring back to Taba, I put the two-inch cutting in a small plastic bag and moistened it with some of the water I had taken from the well.

Back home, I put it in a wineglass with more of the water from the well and within two weeks it started to sprout a leaf. I consulted Silkstone rose-growing expert, Tom Horsfield. Under his expert eyes, the cutting sprang to life within a month. From two inches it soon grew to nine feet. We had been told at the monastery that it grows in no other place and that no cuttings had ever worked, yet here it was thriving. Their famous Bush never flowers and this was thought to be due to its age. At Tom's nursery it has never flowered, but has continued to grow and is still there today.

Some people have questioned my act in taking the cutting and growing the plant in Silkstone. I put the question to some clergy, who failed to give an opinion, but the Bishop of Pontefract at the time, the Rt. Reverend John Finney, told me without hesitation: 'If you do not exploit it, there is nothing wrong.' Priests have meditated at the Bush, children studying scripture have called to see it, people have been turned to Christianity because of it and the BBC called me for permission to use the story on the Terry Wogan 'Thought for the Day' spot.

As far as the right to grow it in Silkstone, I can only think that if God had not wanted it to grow locally it would have perished.

Father Clifford Andrews, the first person from Monk Bretton Church to be ordained, became a great friend along with his wife Ila after a visit to the parish as locum when he conducted fifteen funerals and a wedding in two weeks. A former miner, dapper and colourful Father Andrews invited me to New York to talk about what his people felt was a living part of the Bible.

Of those who question their faith at unsettled times in their lives I ask:

'Why has a monastery surrounded by people of other faiths, and the Bush existed for over 2,000 years?'

It does make one think.

During his visit to Barnsley in 1998, international evangelist Luis Palau said he had heard about my 'Burning Bush' story, and took photographs back to America. In February 2000, Pope John Paul II visited the Bush.

Along the Fairways

T ed Madeley lived in Cudworth, but was a member of a well-known Royston family, having a tailor and outfitter's shop in Midland Road. He was a keen golfer and was the person responsible for introducing me to what has become one of my favourite hobbies. Like the majority of local golfers, he was a member of the Municipal Golf Club at Staincross which, at that time, was run by Barnsley Council yet was in the West Riding County Council area.

It was the early post war years and just like the war years, there was no equipment for any sport. Ted gave me an old golf bag, a few clubs and balls and set me off along the fairways which have brought so much joy and friendship ever since.

Harold Gabbitas was superintendent at the club, being responsible for both the clubhouse and course, and with very little equipment and a staff of three for the 18-hole course at his disposal.

The clubhouse was a former wartime ARP centre and the old wooden clubhouse was used for storage. The course had just come into use after the far nine holes had been released from food production by the Ministry of Agriculture and Fisheries.

Harold was joined by his father, the retired groundsman of Wath Cricket Club, and they did a great job in difficult circumstances. There was no professional at the club, although Barnsley and District Golf club (now Silkstone GC) had Dick Kemp as professional-greenkeeper. Everything was scarce and the majority of players won their golf balls on a gaming machine on the clubhouse bar.

Harold Gabbitas

Harold had good contacts at Slazengers, then based at Horbury Junction, who made clubs for the famous Bobby Locke. He would go on Friday afternoons to Horbury and return with reject clubs which had black painted shafts – chrome was not allowed – and we would queue to buy woods at £2 10s (£2.50) a time. My first set of second hand clubs cost £5.

Harold Gabbitas had 'Fluffy', a black cat, to follow him on the golf course. The cat would ride on his trolley, sit on his shoulder when he

Fluffy rides on Harold's caddycar, and golfer and cat at the 19th hole.

was making a shot and sit and watch when he was putting. When the ball went in the hole, 'Fluffy' would get it out and at the nineteenth hole Harold would enjoy a beer while the cat sipped milk from a saucer.

The Municipal Club had a thriving rabbit golfers' section, run by John Bates and Lance Littlefair and the proudest day in its history was in June 1959 when it staged the Wakefield and District Rabbit Golfers' Association 'Lancaster Trophy' competition. It was the first

The victorious Lancaster Trophy team, myself, Joe Horsfall, Ted Bird and Joe Watling, with, centre, Lance Littlefair and John Bates.

Ted McQuillan hands me the rabbits' section captain's tie.

time it had been held in Barnsley and Harold Gabbitas, his staff, and the council, prepared an excellent course. At the time an observer said: 'This course has never looked better.'

With an aggregate net score of 282, the Municipal team were winners, bringing the trophy to Barnsley for the first time. The team was Joe Horsfall, Joe Watling, Ted Bird and I. Starter for the competition was club character Gilbert Bray, famous for the amount of Jubilee Stout he could drink.

The club had a management committee and members at times attended meetings at the Town Hall with the estates committee which managed the course. Chairmen included Alderman Walter Hunt and Cllr Ron Skelly. The annual meeting was held in the clubhouse, attended by a few councillors, and Harold always made sure the first tee and the 18th green were in prime condition.

Councillors rarely went out onto the course to inspect things, but on one occasion accepted a challenge to play golf.

They were initiated into the game in more ways than one and it rained. The idea of the game was to improve liaison between the club and council and the Mayor, Cllr George Burkinshaw arrived at 2.00pm on a Saturday afternoon in the civic car which was making its first visit to the club. The civic team was dressed in its best attire and after introduction to members of the club team, went to the first tee in heavy rain.

There was no problem recognising the teams, for while the club team had that professional look, the visitors had the same clothing as they had travelled from the Town Hall - worsted suits, soft shoes, felt hats and no weatherproofs.

The civic team included Alderman William Gill and Alderman Edward McVie who had the benefit of the captaincy of John Gibb, a council official who was also the 1953 to 1954 club captain. They defied the weather and got off to a good start. The Mayor, making his first stroke, a good straight 170-yard drive to the first green, but this was not recorded - he was just demonstrating for a photographer.

There was a feeling they would not complete two holes, but the visitors were determined and completed nine holes. They returned to the clubhouse soaked to the skin, defeated, but a team of wiser men.

Cllr Burkinshaw who, like his team mates, set out with two handicaps - a golf handicap and a lack of knowledge - told me after the game:

> *'It was worth it. It was a grand experience, and had Barnsley football team not been at home, we would have had a stronger team.'*

My interest in golf and the weekly golf column in the *Chronicle*, created interest among staff, and soon advertising manager Roy Gill, works manager Ted Bird, and works staff Jack Bradley, Ken Oxley, Granville Wilson, Tommy Taylor, Clive Gill and Jack Wilkinson took up the sport.

My golfing hero was the South African, Bobby Locke who always wore plus-four trousers, a white cap and a collar and tie. He was a portly figure and on two occasions played rounds at the municipal course where, on the tee, he could always be heard asking politely: 'Stand back to the right, please.' He would always push out his shot to the right of the target.

Golf was popular with press people and the county had its own Open Championship. With Roy Gill, I played in the competition at Crosland Heath, Huddersfield, and was declared winner in 1959, but the next morning in the *Yorkshire Post* another competitor was named winner. I received a letter saying I had been disqualified for not signing my card. The following year at Woodthorpe, Wakefield, I came second, but would have won if I had called at the municipal clubhouse and seen

Norman Race and myself with the Garner Rosebowls we won at Silkstone Club's foursomes' event.

that I had received a shot back on my handicap. The following year I made sure everything was in order and won the Yorkshire Press Open Championship at Sand Moor, Leeds.

Holes in one are more luck than skill and on 25 January 1992, I scored my first at the 125-yard ninth at Silkstone GC.

The earliest game I played was at the *Machrie Hotel* and Golf Links on the stunning Isle of Islay, off Scotland's west coast. It was at 5.30am along with three golf fanatics from Japan's Toyota Motor Company. They were still playing when I left them at 8.00am for breakfast.

Jaguar Cars decided to launch a new model at Skibo Castle, Dornoch, which Peter De Savary has used to establish the Carnegie Club. Andrew Carnegie used Skibo as his Highland Castle and described it as 'heaven on earth'. The Scottish-born American steel tycoon left Scotland at the age of thirteen and returned as the richest and most successful man of his generation.

When I arrived there was a huge visitors' book to sign and in the very early pages were the names of King Edward VII, the Rockefellers, Rudyard Kipling, Edward Elgar, Paderewski, Lloyd George, Helen Keller and Sam Torrance, who was married there. The accommodation was outstanding and Edwardian, and my bathroom had a bath on wheel tracks so it could be wheeled out into the bedroom in front of the fire.

Before dinner or early morning, the giant organ in the reception hall would be played and there were no telephone early morning calls - a strolling bagpipe player's music did the trick at 7.00am.

Peter de Savary, the multi-millionaire famous for his America Cup sailing involvement, let me borrow his golf gear to play his new reconstructed course completed by Donald Steel. On later visits to the Castle by Chrysler UK and Ford, he joined me for a round.

Golf is the finest relaxation for the journalist who has a hectic life, and those who have shared my hours on the fairways have been Norman, Stanley and Frank Race, Maurice Kaye, Herbert Taylor, comedian Charlie Williams, Jack Worman, Tom Wilson, Jack Walker, Eric Johnson, Fred Haigh and the late Cyril Dyson.

Standing on the most famous golf bridge in the world, Swilken Bridge, at the Old Course, St Andrew's, Scotland. Jack Nicklaus waved goodbye to The Open from the bridge in July 2000.

Spiritual Journey

Christianity and church life have formed a major part of my life, and my beliefs have helped in my profession and travels around the world - sometimes in dangerous circumstances. My first church was Smithies Wesleyan Reform, where I attended with my neighbour, Jean Hardy, whose family went to the church. After a year I transferred to Old Mill Wesleyan Reform Church, a tiny stone-built chapel, which was part of a small community resting between the railway line and the *Tollgate Hotel*. The chapel was run by a big man, Billy Horbury, who was a warehouseman at Brady Webster's grocery.

My first Sunday school teacher was Elsie Wainwright. The class met in the mornings between 10.00am and 11.00am, and in the afternoons, between 2.00pm and 3.00pm. We dashed out as soon as the clock struck the hour. Things I remember about the chapel are the tiny marble font, which was kept in a glass-fronted case on a window bottom, and the giant, tiered stage which was erected each summer for the anniversary services celebrating the founding of the church. We were given poems to recite in front of family and friends, but I rarely remembered my lines. It was this forced feeding of poetry which in later years killed my liking for this form of expression. The weather for the anniversary was always very warm and the heat made things uncomfortable for those on the top tier of the stage with their heads just below the ceiling. The anniversary was held two weeks before Whitsuntide, which meant all the scholars were allowed to wear their best Whitsuntide dresses, suits and shoes, two weeks early. A jug of water and a glass rested near the pulpit, because someone always fainted through nerves or excessive heat.

My class friends at Burton Road School included Eddie Athorn, Geoffrey Holmes and Peter Haigh and they asked me to join them at St Paul's Church, Monk Bretton, where they were members of the choir. I went along when the vicar was the legendary Father John Alban Edward Mercer, who had arrived in the village in 1919. He was a bachelor, and I was puzzled why they called him 'Father', not realising it was 'high church'. He filled the church morning and evening with his dramatic sermons. People came from the surrounding villages and had to arrive early to get a seat.

Father Mercer left for Cantley, near Doncaster, in 1939 and within a few months Father George Hodgson arrived. There was an excellent

Sunday school in the church hall run by 'Daisey' Bayley and Betty Roberts. I still recall the collection hymn 'Hear the Pennies Dropping'. Father Hodgson was soon called up as an army padre so we had two priests-in-charge, Father Geoffrey Hackett, who prepared me for confirmation, followed by Father Richard Peter Hathaway. It was wartime and Father Hathaway was great with the young lads, donning football kit and joining us for games in the field behind the church and using a football case filled with newspapers on Friday nights for games in the church hall.

He gave us wonderful spiritual guidance with a sporting touch. At the end of the war he too became an army chaplain.

Father Hodgson and his family returned to the vicarage, and the choir got more members. During the war years, when church organist Ernest Exley was with ENSA, Donald Sellars would walk from Kingstone, or Harold Willshie would walk from Barnsley to play the organ. Harold, I remember, would operate the organ pedals in his bare feet.

The choir at St Paul's was in the organ gallery, so was not part of the altar procession. This changed when we received white ruffles with black cassocks. We then walked with the vicar and servers from the vestry. Sam Hadfield was in charge. He taught us where to stand and how to serve the bread and wine to the priest. He also showed us how to light the six huge altar candles. This was a tricky task because, if the wicks had been pressed down when last extinguished, they could be difficult to light. We attended the mass in the morning and the evensong and sermon. As teenagers, I must admit, we found evensong a bit boring, so we would take a book to read during the sermon. Frank Taylor's dad was in the Royal Air Force and sent tins of American peanuts from the NAAFI. Frank would bring a tin to evensong and would slide it along the book rest in the choir stalls for all to share.

One summer's day in the vestry we found what appeared to be a bottle of communion wine. We thought we would take a sip, but the Lord caught us out. It was not wine, but oil used in the sanctuary lamps. We had to dash outside to be sick.

We had a youth club and a busy social life all linked to the church. Christmas and Easter were very important, and every server attended the Christmas midnight mass, which was followed by a party. We had a concert party which toured local churches raising money. Sam Hadfield, who chain-smoked Craven A, was producer and compere, Ronnie Sharpe was the accompanist whose solo spot was 'In a Persian Market', and Lawrence Pritchard played piano accordion. I played drums and offered a trumpet solo. There was also an attractive chorus line with Beryl Cooke, Jean Buttery, Audrey Pitcher, Vera Hewitt,

Alice Pepper and Joan Lisle. At one church their dancing routines caused the stage to move. Highlights were Beryl Cooke's singing of 'Waltzing' and a cowboy sing-song with the lads wearing Scout hats.

Guest appearances were made by a comedian who was a fitter at Monk Bretton pit. He dressed as a vicar. Arthur Batty added a bit of class with violin solos.

St Paul's Church formed a major part of my young life and when Father William Jubb moved from Royston to be vicar, I became a sidesman and member of the Church Council. It was my first taste of church administration, and I was shocked to find the average age of the Church Council was seventy-three!

Harry Athorn and Lloyd Ward were wardens, and when Harry died I took over his post which I have now held for thirty-four years.

Father Jubb was faced with major church renovation and only his financial skills made it possible to complete the tasks. He left in 1974 and at the same time there was an exodus with Lloyd Ward retiring

Father William Jubb, Vicar of Monk Bretton for 22 years, resigned from the living in July 1974. He had raised thousands of pounds for the church through bingo sessions, collecting waste paper and other events. His financial expertise kept the church door open. A year after he resigned, he was divorced and three days later married former Sunday School superintendent and church secretary, Liz Ellis at Barnsley Registry Office. He remained in the village and died in November 1999, seven months before they would have celebrated their silver wedding. His funeral service was held in the church he had served so well. He is seen with Liz in a relative's garden.

Father Jubb makes a presentation to long-serving organist Ernest Exley, watched by veteran church council members and myself.

as warden, Liz Ellis as Sunday School superintendent and secretary and also treasurer, Eric Thornton, who moved to another village. I was alone after only a few years as warden, but found great strength in Rural Dean, Canon John Brumpton. Not only did he have our problem, but also the famous exorcism incident at Gawber.

Problems mounted, but the small congregation gave me every support and eventually Ernest Horbury was also made warden and Brain and Lorraine Wells became treasurers. There were so many problems that my family never had a holiday in 1974.

There were also problems getting possession of the vicarage and Bishop Eric Treacy gave an instruction to the Rural Dean and wardens. He said: 'Break in and change the locks.' We wondered what explanation we should give if caught in the act.

Bishop Treacy then announced he had found a new vicar in Father Howard Crosthwaite, but he withdrew his acceptance of the living and we went back to square one.

It was during this period the mysteries of church administration were revealed in all their glory. If Canon Brumpton and I had not enjoyed a regular sherry and looked at the funny side then I am sure we would both have ended up going over the top. His wife would often call, at times in tears, and ask for some action because church problems were making him ill. In one circumstance I was even offered £25,000 by a national newspaper to reveal everything that I knew. I refused. They argued that my allegiance was to journalism. However I said it was to the church.

Eventually Father Harold Ingamells arrived in May 1975, and he found a church ripe for development. His style of worship initially was popular, and his first harvest festival was a packed house in both church and hall. He liked the charismatic renewal form of worship and that brought my first experience of a church 'split'. Many people did not like this type of worship which was promoted by Bishop Richard Hare. It was bright and uplifting worship, but the majority wanted the traditional Anglo-Catholic ways.

One service he was to attend was advertised in the *Chronicle* as 'the Bishop from Wakefield', but when people arrived they were annoyed because it was the Bishop of Pontefract, Richard Hare. He was jostled in the aisle by a few protesters and I was accused of misinforming them in the paper. This was untrue, because Bishop Hare did live in Wakefield (not Pontefract) and the paper's report 'Bishop from Wakefield' was correct. It was my first taste of how stupid opinions came before Christianity.

Father Ingamells was still vicar when in 1978 the church

celebrated its centenary. I wrote the first history of the church and the booklet sold out in two weeks, raising £700 for the restoration appeal. Rather unique on the celebration day was the attendance of Gertrude Atkinson and Bertha Fox, both 100 years old, making it a treble centenary celebration. Later another of my booklets raised £2,500 for church floodlights.

When Father Ingamells left we had another lengthy interregnum until a Stevenage curate, Father Richard Hoyle, was appointed. His institution was however to be conducted by Bishop Hare because Bishop Colin James had phoned to say he couldn't make it. When on the phone I had said in confidence that I thought it was a bad idea that Bishop Hare should come as in the past there had been strong opposition to his churchmanship from the congregation. When Bishop Hare arrived he was not happy and it soon became apparent that he had been told of my objection. He called me into a room along with warden Clifford Bullock to discuss the matter where he expressed his dissatisfaction – and that's putting it mildly. It taught me that some clergy do not like some outspoken church wardens or Church Council members who are only trying to express the views of the people they represent. I thought I was protecting Father Hoyle early in his ministry.

The post of church warden is not only a church appointment, but a village appointment carrying many responsibilities and legal standing. Wardens are also the bishop's representatives and each year swear allegiance.

During Father Hoyle's time the church was split again when he tried to introduce lay administration of the chalice. It was a near 50-50 split and I was criticised for supporting the protesters. I did this because they had no one by their side and, if not represented, would have left the church. Administration by the laity did come into operation, but many would only take the bread from the priest and not the wine from a lay person (a non-cleric). The problem was not completely resolved and again this brought heartache to my family. People would call at our home, some in tears, all because of the chalice issue. They valued the sacraments as the height of their belief and felt only a priest should administer them.

Father Hoyle left for Ilkley and it was during the next interregnum that a group of youths broke into the vicarage garage where the communion wine had been stored. They drank the lot and I found four of them drunk in the vicarage gardens singing 'We plough the fields and scatter'.

Father Christopher Irving was the next vicar and it was not long before all but a few members of the congregation were accepting wine from laity. His period included the planning and building of the £165,000 church centre, after we had sold the old church hall to

Mencap. We also sold the curate's house in Coronation Street which gave us a good financial start. A City Challenge grant of £20,000 also helped to make the project possible, a grant supported by Cllr Charles Wraith, against opposition from some people who said the church was outside the catchment area.

We worked for a year planning the centre, and another year supervising its construction, but 11 November 1992, became a sad day for St Paul's Church, and some would say also for the Church of England. It was the day the General Synod voted in favour of women priests. Father Irving was very much an opponent of women priests and made the fact well known to the Church Council and congregation. The Church Council agreed with him and passed resolutions banning women priests in the church and not accepting the Episcopal oversight of the Diocesan Bishop, Nigel McCulloch.

Several churches in the Barnsley area, known as the 'biretta belt' because of the prominence of high churchmanship, did the same. There was much unrest, and Bishop Nigel, because he had voted in favour of women priests, was not welcome over the threshold at St Paul's Church.

By church law, no one could stop him visiting a church because he was Diocesan Bishop, but the only time he came to Monk Bretton was by invitation to a Church Council meeting when I, and not the vicar, was chairman. He was surprised he met with no aggression.

Bishop Nigel is an inspiring person wherever he goes and much loved by churchgoers. The church could not have a finer person to promote the word of God in ways they understand.

There are times in life when one's beliefs are tested, and as a church warden mine were tested many times. After the chalice issue, I had made up my mind that never again would I get involved in church controversy. As a Christian, I felt one could do better with time, talents and money than fight over the issue of women priests.

On Remembrance Day, 1995, Bishop Nigel returned to Monk Bretton to celebrate mass at St Paul's Church and to conduct the service at the village war memorial. He later attended a service at the Methodist Church. He concluded his visit by joining the Royal British Legion and club members at a reception at West Green Working Men's Club. His presence was appreciated by villagers.

During the period without a vicar, the Church Council had to reconsider the three

A bound volume of my Chronicle *feature 'Do You Need Your Parish Church?', was taken to Bishop's Lodge and handed to the Archbishop of Canterbury, Robert Runcie.*

resolutions concerning women priests. I felt the one concerning episcopal oversight was so un-Christian that I said I would resign if it was not rescinded. It was agreed to do that. In the year 2000 I feel there are still 'hidden' strong feelings in the diocese on this issue. There may be smiles and handshakes, but are they genuine?

'Flying Bishop' John Gaisford, appointed to oversee parishes not prepared to accept the Diocesan Bishop, was one of the kindest clergymen I had met. It was a pity we did not share the same views, but I do respect those who share them with him.

There was always a fear that a priest would not arrive for a wedding or funeral, because I had at the back of my mind an incident 20 years earlier when the cortege for the late Ford Ashton had been left at the church gates for 45 minutes when the priest was late. While he was being collected by car, I had to enter the church by the back door and set up the coffin stands and books, allowing undertaker Michael Hadfield an opportunity to console the family.

After that incident, I always attended a funeral with a service book and prepared universal address just in case I had to conduct the service. Any citizen may conduct a funeral service.

Father Ron Letall and I had to deal with the biggest funerals seen at the church since the one for Manchester United and England forward Tommy Taylor, who was killed in the Munich Air Disaster. The church was filled to capacity for the funeral of 13-year-old Kate Ward, who had died from cancer. Over 200 of her school friends at Willowgarth High School each carried a red rose as they entered church and later filled her grave with roses.

Within the space of three months the church could not accommodate the mourners for two young people. Paul Broughton, a 16-year-old who lived in Burton Road, Monk Bretton, was killed in a road accident and because his favourite colour was purple, his family decided he should have a purple coffin. At the service was his friend, 22-year-old Andrew McNamara, who told Father Letall that

Bishop of Wakefield, the Rt Revd Nigel McCulloch, was given a very friendly welcome at the institution of Father John Morrison-Wells in 1997. Father Irving left Monk Bretton and later became a Roman Catholic priest.

he was so impressed with the service, that when he died he wanted the same church and priest.

Three months later, Andrew, also of Burton Road, was killed in a car accident in Rotherham Road. His coffin was black, his favourite colour. They both had discos at their funeral services. Michael Hadfield had carried out the wishes of the families.

It was the first time permission had been given for such music, but we decided if it pleased the families that was the most important point. The congregations were so big, mourners filled the aisles, chancel and even sat on the chancel floor. Others stood in the churchyard.

It is impossible to reflect the life of a person in a 20-minute crematorium service and a church is still the best place. A funeral should not be depressing and many request cassettes were played of the person's favourite music. The demand was so great we had to install a cassette player and Frank Sinatra sang 'I did it my way' more times in Monk Bretton church than he did on Broadway. We felt if families wanted this way to pay their last respects, it should be allowed. No matter how sad, the majority would say 'It was a good funeral'.

One unusual request we had was for a recording to be played of the deceased singing in his bath. But the family were happy.

Humour crept into services and at a baptism service the wardens had to deal with a man who would not refrain from smoking and another who came for the service dressed in just his vest and trousers. A youngster also shocked the congregation by going down the aisle for a blessing in a pair of 'flashing boots' which, at that time, were the craze.

At a wedding the groom's father could not be found and a search was made. The ceremony went ahead and midway through a chap in tailcoat and top hat walked through the curtains at the back of the church. I asked if he was the groom's father and, with alcohol-laden breath that overpowered me, he said he was, but had missed the taxi. When I offered to take him to his place he said he would prefer to stand outside, until I explained he should walk down the aisle with the bride's mother at the end of the service. He straightened his white carnation and I slipped him into a side aisle pew. The guests turned and smiled at this rosy-cheeked family member, who, seconds later, walked down the aisle with the mother - as though he had been there all the time.

Early one Sunday morning a mother telephoned with a request for her daughter to be married at the church. I said there would be no problem, but she said she was living in Japan to which I said she may need an archbishop's certificate. But then she said the bridegroom was Japanese and his father wanted to wear his kimono and carry a ceremonial sword. The kimono, I said, was all right, but the sword was not. With special documentation, including a letter from the Japanese embassy, the wedding went ahead in grand style.

Midweek services do not escape incident. At one evening mass, two youngsters came down the aisle on roller-skates.

Above the church pulpit is a large crucifix which was donated by the White family, but one Good Friday when it was used on the altar for the veneration of the cross, it was knocked to the chancel floor and smashed into hundreds of pieces. A repair looked impossible, but my daughter Julie and I gathered the bits and spread them on our garage floor. We used superglue to put the trunk together and gave the body a spine of old printer's brass rules. We pieced together all the small parts and remoulded the statue with polyfiller. Jesus was then painted in dulux brilliant white emulsion.

Miracles do happen, because this statue did rise again, but we could not remove a 'wound' mark in his right side. It is still there...where he was jabbed with a spear by the soldiers.

Vandalism was always a problem until during a game of golf I met Grant Doyle, who headed a local security firm. He offered a daily patrol free of charge and this led to television, radio and newspaper publicity. After my interview on BBC Radio Sheffield, a listener sent me £1,200 towards repairing vandalism damage. One newspaper described it as 'Tenners from Heaven'.

St Paul's Church does a tremendous job serving a community of more than 20,000. It is fortunate to have so many capable lay workers not only to serve the church, but raise money to keep open its doors.

A parish without a vicar causes problems. It makes life hectic for all involved with the church as retired priests from surrounding parishes are drafted in to lend their support. At one time in Monk Bretton we went 20 months without a vicar, and only help from Father Ron Letall, Peter Ainsworth, Derek Birch and Mel Garside made services possible. An empty vicarage can also be a problem. Once, three weeks after the vicar had left, thieves entered the vicarage and ransacked the place. Each evening it was my job to check the rooms. One day the postman rang to say that he could smell gas outside the vicarage. I went to investigate and found that the gas meters and boiler had all been stolen and that the thieves had turned the gas supply on. I called the gas emergency service who found that the build up of gas was such that the house could blow up at any time. We evacuated the area and part of the roof was removed to release the gas. The gas emergency service said that the build up was so high that even someone turning on a torch could have ignited the place. I realised I had been very fortunate the night before by not turning on a light when I had checked the place. Although many people look upon St Paul's Church, as their spiritual home, they do not realise it costs £600 a week to run.

Spiritual involvement did not only surround St Paul's Church, but also in the Wakefield Diocese where I served the communications committee under three bishops, and in 1985 was invited to join a small group with Michael Kinchin-Smith, the Archbishop's Appointments Secretary and Robin Catford, the Prime Minister's Appointments Secretary, to express views about the diocese and the sort of person we would like to see as the next Bishop of Wakefield. Later David Hope became Bishop of Wakefield, then Bishop of London and now Archbishop of York.

In January 1994 I was invited by the Bishop's Council to join the newly formed Diocesan Vision and Strategy Group, with the aim of looking at the diocese and all levels of church life. The chairperson was Baroness Jean McFarlane; vice chairman, the Rt Reverend John Finney, Bishop of Pontefract; Dr Keri Thomas, Canon Richard Giles, the Reverend Trevor Hicks, the Reverend Kit Widdows, the Reverend Margaret Smith, Maureen Browell, Geoffrey France, John McLeod and myself. Working with the group was very satisfying and a wonderful spiritual experience.

Being a church warden makes it possible to help people of all denominations in many ways and it is a satisfying public appointment. During an interview on BBC Radio Sheffield in 1998 I was asked if it had been difficult being an editor with Christian beliefs. No, was my answer.

About this time I published my own Ten Commandments which are valuable in life and human relationships, just like the Bible commandments. They are just as important as I write this chapter:

1. Speak to people. There is nothing as nice as a cheerful greeting.
2. Call people by name - not names. The sweetest music is to hear one's name called.
3. Have humility. There is something to be learned from every living thing.
4. Be friendly. If you have a friend - be one.
5. Be cordial. Speak and act as if everything you do is a pleasure.
6. Be interested in others. You can like almost everybody if you try.
7. Be generous with praise and cautious with criticism.
8. Give your word, then keep it.
9. Be considerate of the feeling of others.
10. Be alert to give service. What counts most in life is what we do for others.

Editor's Chair

The 1984 to 1985 miners' strike took its toll on the *Chronicle*, like any other local business. Advertising revenue and sales of the paper were badly hit, weekly circulation dropped from around 40,000 to just over 33,000 copies within the year. The strike was correctly described as 'the bitterest 12 months in Britain's postwar industrial history'.

On 13 January 1986, I was appointed editor of the *Chronicle*, following a journey from the front counter to the top editorial chair of Yorkshire's best-selling weekly newspaper. It was a great honour, but a difficult job to tackle because sales had only just started to recover by a few copies each week.

The editor of a weekly may be far removed in salary and influence from that of the editor of a national or regional newspaper, but he has his own niche in the journalistic gallery and has reached the top of one of the many newspaper ladders. He has his own responsibilities and they make a specialised demand upon his professional knowledge and skills.

Again I found it difficult to settle in a more managerial post because, like so many journalists, I preferred the daily chase for news, with the never-ending variety of experiences which it brings, rather than the more ordered routine of an 'indoor job'. As a reporter, each day arriving at the office held a mystery. The next person to be met or place to be visited was not known. As an editor, the most important task was to watch for any legal difficulties that surrounded news stories and avoid slip-ups in employment legislation when dealing with staff.

The whole business of newspapers has been ruined in the past twenty years by the power of the company accountants and so-called marketing experts. Usually, they have no idea what is the life-blood of newspapers, yet their ideas are accepted. Of course, the same push for profits is present in other business concerns. I feel, however, that weekly newspapers are something special and form an important part of the community. They become part of the family and usually are around in the house for six days, whereas a daily paper lasts less than twenty-four hours.

The editorial and business departments at the *Chronicle* were poles apart at times and on occasions there was active antagonism, which cannot be good for any newspaper. There was a major development of the advertising side of the newspaper, which eventually brought in more money than actual newspaper sales. After having only one sales representative, Dave Parkin, the *Chronicle* sales department expanded rapidly. Originally, only the editor would have a company car, but by the 1980s the *Chronicle* had a fleet, mainly for advertising representatives. Colin Day was Group Advertising Manager and he and I had regular clashes when his huge adverts filled up, what I considered to be, valuable editorial space.

We had a good working relationship which was probably unique in the newspaper world, for the editor must always fight to resist threats to his editorial space from advertising.

The advertising budgets, to me as an editor, seemed unrealistic, but the field sales representatives did do a remarkable job. The saviour of weekly newspapers was not only property and motoring advertising, but also special features for manufacturing concerns.

An editor needs the support of his staff and in many ways I was fortunate in this respect, but, like so many managers, there were some weeks when the majority of my time seemed to be spent dealing with staff welfare problems and complaints from readers about their pet hates.

Reporters can be collecting news in a back street one minute and attending courts and meetings where dignity is important the next. I always requested that staff dress smartly and that men wear collars and ties, not loose fitting shirts and jerseys. They never let me down. Some editors were envious of the adherence of *Chronicle* staff to the dress rules.

Although each week I would receive numerous letters from people wanting a career in journalism, it was difficult to find the right people because many did not realise that it was not a nine to five job. Also, those with university or college training did not always prove the best and there were good recruits like Alan Whitehouse, a local lad from grammar school, who came with great enthusiasm, then spent some years with the *Yorkshire Post* and is now the BBC Transport Correspondent. Nick Ward, at thirty-plus, asked for a job because no other paper in South Yorkshire would consider him. He had been made redundant from the steel industry twice, but was so keen to become a journalist that he financed himself through college. He was so enthusiastic I offered him a job, but could only pay him £120 a week, which was very poor in the early 1990s for a married man with a child, so I allowed him to enhance his weekly expenses to help pay for his petrol each day from Sheffield to Barnsley and back. Nick was a good investment because he proved his worth and later I was able to increase his wage. He became 'Yorkshire Journalist of the Year' and now works for the *Sheffield Star*. Many young reporters and photographers were given their first step on the newspaper ladder at the *Chronicle*.

After only two months in the editor's chair, I faced my first case of union militancy from Barnsley branch members of the National Union of Journalists. For fifteen years the *Chronicle's* 'Girl Friday' feature of local lovelies had proved very popular with teenagers and parents. It was then stopped when the photographers failed to keep up a good supply of pictures. I had many requests to re-start the feature which did not include scantily-clad or topless girls, but swim suits or dresses.

Mike Noon, the NUJ secretary, really planned his campaign and copies of the letter he sent to me were also sent to the UK *Press Gazette* (weekly magazine). The *Journalist* (the NUJ's monthly newspaper) and the *Campaign for Press and Broadcasting Freedom*. That brought requests for comments, which I gave and this brought forth headlines in magazines such as 'Chapel fumes over editor's beauty pictures'. A 'Chapel' is a trade union group within a newspaper. The union chaps felt that in the light of recent rape cases and growing public outrage, my comments were particularly ill-timed and insensitive. It was also claimed that no attention had been paid to photographers' claims that some of the girls featured had received obscene telephone calls. That was found to be true in a few instances, so subsequently addresses were omitted from the feature and there were no further problems. Other newspapers also started to omit addresses and 'Girl Friday' and even 'Man Friday' features continued to be a big success, with more requests to the featured.

Publishing names and addresses in the *Chronicle* became a serious problem, not only with teenagers, but also with children and pensioners and eventually I stopped using the addresses of children to avoid possible approaches of paedophiles.

On one occasion we helped the regional crime squad, along with the aid of a criminal psychologist, to trap a sex nuisance who had in his possession files of children following their appearances in newspapers and magazines. It was just one instance where a newspaper can help the community.

Obscene calls would not only be made to the young, but also the elderly and one day a woman telephoned to say she was being pestered by telephone calls 'because she had worn a tight blouse' in her golden wedding photograph published in the paper. We trapped him, too.

Letters to the editor are the heart of a newspaper and at one period the *Chronicle* failed to make good use of readers' submissions. Those we did publish were often boring and from contributors who would often demand their letters be published. The same names appeared week after week, mainly on the subjects of politics or religion. The responsibility selecting letters for placement in the paper was often left to a compositor, not a newsman. The number of letters is a barometer of a paper's success, because it shows readers are taking an interest in its contents. Some weeks we had over fifty letters and extra space had to be found to accommodate them. When we published a photo of a topless woman, called Angelina, on the front page, from behind, I might say, more than 100 letters were received in response. Letters were treated as being as important as news and were given a later deadline, enabling readers to comment on the previous week's stories.

The topless Angelina again brought us national magazine cover. She had been engaged to dress as Eve and hand out apples to the public. This was supposed to be a symbol representing the fruit of knowledge. The national tabloid dailies persuaded her to go topless, so, rather than miss the photograph, the *Sun* took a full frontal photograph. The *Chronicle*, however, was happy with the more demure photograph from behind. I decided there was a way to cover this event with the shot from the back. The headline in the UK *Press Gazette* read 'Saucy but suitable for family readership'!

The *Chronicle* became the fourth best-selling weekly newspaper in the country and its exclusive stories were frequently used by national newspapers. In fact, they could not wait for Friday so that they could use our stories, often without even checking with us first.

One of its greatest achievements came after a visit to the *Chronicle* offices by the Russian cosmonaut, Lt Col Alexander Volkov, from Barnsley's Soviet twin town, Gorlovka. The paper had a cartoon character, Sam Barn, who appeared in a feature, 'The Ascent of Sam', drawn by the paper's artist, Roni Wilkinson. Sam was so popular there were knitted models of the character and on his office tour assistant editor, Ian Thompson, asked the Russian to take Sam on his next trip into space on the Mir space station.

The following Christmas, the BBC decided to have a live link-up with the space craft on the programme *Christmas Morning with Noel Edmonds*. It was beamed down to millions throughout the world. During the interview, conducted through an interpreter in the BBC studio, Noel Edmonds asked:

> *'Can you tell me, what is that thing floating around – that the Commander is holding? Is it a good luck emblem of some sort?'*

The three of us, Alexander Volkov, the Russian cosmonaut, Sam Barn and myself, before the famous space flight.

At times, letters from readers arrived by the sackful.

Lt Col Volkow replied:

> 'This is a doll that came from Barnsley, England. It is a humorous character from the Barnsley Chronicle. Happy Christmas to the people of Barnsley and Chronicle readers.'

At a time when Barnsley was trying to improve its image after the miners' strike and attract new industry, the publicity was priceless.

It was the greatest free world-wide publicity Barnsley has ever received and originated at the *Chronicle*.

Possibly unknown to Barnsley's Labour councillors – they thought

BBC Radio Sheffield's Roni Robinson on one of his many visits.

I was against them – I did everything possible to support their work to regenerate the area. In the Irish Republic, at a Mercedes-Benz conference, the head of the German company said there was a possibility that the new factory for its first small car, the A-Class, would be built in the UK. A fax was sent to council leader Hedley Salt with the news because I thought that, with their commercial base at Tankersley, we might also capture the car factory. He immediately contacted Stuttgart but, after pressure from the German trade unions, the car was made in Germany.

The *Chronicle's* standing in the world of weekly newspapers brought constant demands from television and radio programmes for special features. We were included in 'The Editors' television programme and media writer Brian MacArthur was regularly on the telephone and writing in the *Sunday Times* said:

'You learn much more about the real lives of the people of England from reading the Barnsley Chronicle or any other paid-for weeklies than from any national paper.'

He liked the story of Batmania and S.R. Gent winning an exclusive contract with Warner Bros. and Marks and Spencer to supply Batman clothes, producing 10,000 garments a week. Yet he also spotted the paper had found room on its front page for a picture of a boy of three who had grown an eleven-foot beanstalk.

Roni Robinson, of BBC Radio Sheffield, was a regular visitor to my office to broadcast live programmes, even when the paper was redesigned. On one occasion he helped the engineer to arrange the cables through the office window. It gave me a chance to take a quick look at his clipboard. Among the questions the producer had listed was 'get Booker involved in politics'. They knew politics came at the bottom of my list of interests, but this time I was ready.

Tony Wilkinson spent a week in the office to produce his famous 'Wilko's Weekly' programme for BBC Radio 4. He met many staff, worked on the district editions and when broadcast, the programme was reviewed by Alan Cunningham in the *Mail on Sunday*. He did not think much to my great liking for Barnsley folk and their cloth-cap image. I said I always found them genuine and friendly and he wrote:

'Except on Saturday nights when all thirteen town centre pubs hire bouncers and there's a three-hour wait at the hospital for the victims upholding Barnsley's finest tradition...brawling.'

Judging the baby competition was always a major task.

> '*Even weddings aren't immune. A bridegroom arrived in church wrecked after a stag-night punch up, only to be given another hiding outside the church by his wife after the service. But it's the new kiddy-crime that Don abhors. Like the violence, the razing of two schools - and the theft of all Grimethorpe Colliery Band's instruments. Yet, Wilko, shouting like a ferret into every newsy crevice, finds that up to eight in ten people are jobless in an area that has only three of its forty-two pits left since the 1984 strike. And Grimethorpe had desperate poverty.*'

That's what Alan Cunningham had to say and ironically it was only a few months later that the *Chronicle* scooped the world's press with news that the area's last two pits were to close.

International, national and regional press invaded Barnsley to record the closure of its pits and deputy editor John Threlkeld, with his mining memories and files, was a constant source of information for them. But the *Chronicle* beat them all to an exclusive, due to good contacts and pure journalist's luck.

Within two hours of deadline in the second week of the battle to save the pits, I received a telephone call from the Bishop of Wakefield's chaplain, Roy Clements, with whom I had worked on the

Wakefield Diocesan Communications Committee. There was a swift change to the front page leading story and the *Chronicle* was able to tell readers that its last two pits were to close on 30 October 1992. The news came just a few days after Board of Trade president Michael Heseltine had told the House of Commons the pit closure programme was to be reviewed. Grimethorpe and Houghton Main Collieries were the only pits left in the Barnsley area and just when miners and their families thought there might be a chance of a reprieve, they were told they would be closed within the week.

My source, Roy Clements, had been in conversation with me about another matter only ten minutes before the vital call. Then the chaplain heard from the vicar of Grimethorpe and the bishop, that the local branch of the NUM had been called in to the pit to be told of the closure.

The saying 'stop the front page' became reality and I was able to get letters of protest faxed from the vicar and the bishop, which were all published for the Friday breakfast reading. The regional papers followed hours later, along with radio and television. There was a wonderful team effort throughout the newspaper to beat the other media - even America's *Wall Street Journal*.

The *Chronicle* was always being asked to publicise local charities, but the biggest challenge came with a bid to raise money for a proposed hospice for the terminally ill in the Barnsley area. Every Wednesday Sharad and Sarala Mahatme along with Yvonne Bligh would call at the front office with a list of that week's donations towards a £1 million appeal. It went on for months and around £3,000 was raised.

I felt this was Barnsley's biggest ever need, so decided to make it the paper's major campaign. *Chronicle* senior management were not too happy about the idea because they felt it would fail and this would reflect on the newspaper. But I had faith in local people and launched the Hospice Appeal with a front page leader asking every reader to give £1 to get the appeal on its way. The response was overwhelming and within the first week several thousand pounds were donated. But then nearly every organisation decided they wanted to raise money or make donations. After three months the total had risen to £145,000 and over the years Barnsley was swamped with money-raising events for the hospice.

The appeal, however, did hit a low for four years, but only one person complained. The hospice appeal target had to be achieved. It was named St Peter's Hospice Appeal because our first meeting was in St Peter's Church Hall. I became a director and vice-chairman. We worked ceaselessly, mainly in the hospice office, now the shop, in Eldon Street, sitting through winter meetings of up to five hours duration without proper heating.

There was a continual inflow of money for the fund and each week the *Chronicle* recorded the week's donations in a special feature, often with photographs. But little progress was made towards a building, although the former Pindar Oaks Nursing Home in Sheffield Road, Barnsley and a former school site at Royston were investigated.

Architects said it would be more difficult to adapt, rather than build a new hospice and this became reality when, led by Cllr Hedley Salt, Barnsley Council offered a wonderful site in Church Street, Gawber, for a peppercorn rent and Caroline Amelia Robertson, who had read my initial appeal for £1, contacted Mr Mahatma and left £400,000 in her will.

She was the widow of a former medical professor and had lived in Barnsley only a few years. The gestures of Barnsley Council and Mrs Robertson, along with the kindness of young and old readers and the Mahatma family made today's hospice possible.

For some reason, which I still find difficult to understand, appeal and directors' meetings were surrounded by problems. When a vote of 'no confidence' was put forward against a director, I had to be chairman of the meeting. I was so concerned that I asked my priest at Monk Bretton, Father Irving, to offer a special Friday mass for the meeting, which he did, and the prayers were answered. The meeting went better than expected.

The huge success of the hospice appeal caused concern among other local charities and some wrote to me complaining. They felt it was adversely affecting their appeals, so the *Chronicle* introduced the

The day we cut the first sod for St Peter's Hospice at Gawber. Prayers had been answered.

weekly Charity Chatter column which was compiled by Ian Harley and offered them whatever space they wanted. They were happy.

The first sod at the Gawber site was cut in February 1993 and the day-patient unit accepted its first patients in June 1994.

My faith in the people of Barnsley had been realised and they had dug deep into their pockets to help the terminally ill – there is no greater contribution in life one can make. They are very brave people.

As in all commercial concerns, memos at the *Chronicle* were an important part of daily life, but the following sent by general manager John Bayne, to my office on the subject of the hospice, was heart-warming. It was dated 27 January 1994, and read: 'One cannot start to think of how many memoranda one has received over my years at the *Chronicle* but, without doubt, few have given me such pleasure and pride than the one from you about the success of the hospice appeal.

'My initial warning note nine years ago, was based on genuine concern for you and for the Chronicle. *However, I had reckoned without your strength and purpose in this matter and at that time I did not realise you were so committed to the project and that you would be courageous enough to guarantee with your personal assets to ensure the progress of the hospice. Also, underestimated at that time was the generosity of the people of Barnsley who, encouraged by your continued enthusiasm in the* Chronicle, *have brought about an outstanding achievement. I can only add my heartfelt congratulations to you, the* Chronicle *and the people of Barnsley.'*

The hospice directors had no routine insurance cover if things went wrong and we had to guarantee our assets to get that cover in case any claims were made. We could have lost everything we possessed. Directors Alan Sherriff, who added financial expertise into the project, Keith Lax, Maureen Harrison and Brenda Hinchcliffe worked tirelessly for the scheme. When the latter three were not re-elected at the annual meeting in 1995, Alan Sherriff and I stood down although we had received unanimous votes. On a matter of principle and respect for the disposed directors, I resigned. It was the saddest decision I had ever made and over the years my principles have proved costly.

At the time Clive Cawthrow and Jeff Ennis were the council's observers at meetings.

The hospice still gets my full support, with more than £1,000 from the sale of my local history books being donated, along with fees from all my after-dinner speaking appointments.

At the same time that the hospice appeal was running, I was asked to raise money for the revolutionary key-hole surgery equipment that was required by surgeon Rik Waddington, at the Barnsley District General Hospital. An appeal was mounted and readers responded wonderfully. In three months the £34,000 worth of equipment was handed over. The baby special care and coronary care units also regularly benefited from appeals in the *Chronicle*.

There was a period in the early 1990s when Barnsley carried the tag of 'car crime centre of the UK'. Car thefts reached an all time high, so I banned the description 'joy rider' from the paper, replacing it with 'car thieves'. The thefts increased, but one day when news came in that an invalid at Mapplewell had not only had her car stolen, but the roof had been cut off and her invalid chair thrown into Bretton lake, I felt something had to be done.

A leading article was published on the front page criticising, not the police or magistrates, but the do-gooders in society – and the Community Service Order system – who seemed to give more support to the offender than the victim.

Readers had been expressing a desire for a long time for the return of corporal punishment, in other words the birch, so we tested feeling by offering for the first time in the UK, a telephone voting system. It was used two years later on the same topic by the *Sun* and *Daily Mirror*.

The response was fantastic, with more than 5,000 readers voting in favour of its introduction and only 200 against. So many readers' letters were received that extras pages had to be provided for their publication.

At the time, I had served twelve years as a magistrate and it came to light that my comments on crime had been watched and possibly recorded. I was asked to meet a deputation at Barnsley Magistrates' Court, which included the chairman of the bench, chairman of the advisory committee and Brian Colbeck, deputy clerk to the Justices. I was told the informal meeting had been called at the request of the Lord Chancellor's Office, which had received a letter from the Barnsley Law Society regarding my adjudication on motoring cases following comments in the *Chronicle*. They felt they were prejudicial to me sitting as a magistrate. I was handed the letter which I was seeing for the first time.

The society had sent a photocopy of my *Chronicle* article and the letter said they had been asked by all the local practitioners who practised daily in the court to bring the article to his attention. The letter said:

'*They have grave concerns as to the views openly expressed by Mr Booker. In particular, he appears to indicate that a certain method of disposing of a defendant by imposing a community service upon him as a direct alternative to imprisoning that defendant is a waste of time. Local law practitioners are very concerned about Mr Booker's fitness to continue to serve on the bench given the views that he openly expresses. There are concerns about the quality of the justice to be administered by this magistrate in the future towards their clients.*'
They asked the Lord Chancellor's Department to investigate and if I was proved wrong in expressing the views, 'appropriate steps should be taken to remedy the situation'. In other words, I would be asked to resign.

Unknown to the society, at the time of their complaint, I was on six months' leave of absence from the bench due to major developments at the *Chronicle*, but as the company's solicitor pointed out, I was perfectly entitled to voice a view and it would be contrary to my right of freedom of speech if any attempt was made to gag me.

A London barrister specialising in newspapers, said he had never heard anything like it before and felt it would be a major issue in the UK if I was asked to resign. The British Guild of Editors was waiting in the wings to tackle the Law Society and the country's quality newspapers wanted my story. My respect for the magistracy did not allow me to gain publicity.

Throughout my service on the bench, no solicitor had complained about my decisions and often in motoring cases, I had advised defendants. Magistrates have guidelines and these I always observed. For some reason, the local solicitors had pre-judged the situation, something magistrates are told they must never do. I was not prepared to resign from the bench for I had only expressed the views of readers. The offending article had not even carried my name.

Sporting and political personalities were regular callers seeking publicity, in fact without media attention such people would not be as famous. Some became friends, but in later years when I was of no benefit, that friendship seemed to lapse. Some who never hunted publicity, but deserved more, were world-famous shot-putter Arthur Rowe, Olympic gold medallist Dorothy Hyman and paraplegic Olympic medal winner, Cyril Thomas.

Among my final campaigns was one to rid the town centre of charity cheats, the people with collecting boxes who would gather in Cheapside near the market entrances and near Marks and Spencer. They ostensibly collected for such causes as the hospice, riding for the disabled and the heart-touching 'Children's Leukaemia Appeal'.

In many cases they had not been registered locally and had fake authorisation badges.

Articles in the paper called for police action, but nothing was done, so I contacted Bob Wright, Barnsley Council's Programme Director for Health, Home and Care Services and he quickly sent his staff to investigate. The police then also started to investigate.

These cheats were taking money away from Barnsley's deserving charities. They were found to be operating from the Midlands. The regional crime squad telephoned me to say they had arrested four employees of a private company who were organising the collectors and, on raiding their offices, had found a file containing my name, address and articles I had written.

Then Bob Wright wrote to me with news that after protracted investigations by Nottingham Police a group operating there had been arrested and a seven-month trial ensued. It was hoped to get sufficient evidence to reclaim all monies received by the organisation and hand it over to local charities.

I never got to know the conclusion because the case was not reported locally, but Bob did write:

'The front page article in this matter, for which I must thank you, certainly caught the attention of the Barnsley public, a number of whom later gave witness statements to the police.'

When I decided to have a new horoscope for the paper, famous astrologer Russell Grant called to see me with his column. He walked into my office apologising because he had no shoes, just socks. He explained that he preferred to drive without shoes, and on his journey from Wales with his pet Labrador, the dog had chewed and eaten his shoes in the back of his car. Before continuing his journey to Yorkshire Television in Leeds, he walked in his socks to Barnsley Market to buy a new pair. It was something he had failed to forecast.

The editorship was a powerful post, but things did not always go well. I was wrong to criticise the naming of gardens in Back Regent Street and Hanson Street 'Mandela Gardens'. But my biggest internal fight was against the introduction of the *Chronicle's* 'Heart to Heart' feature. It was strictly a commercial idea, but I felt there was no place in a family newspaper for adverts seeking partners.

I argued strongly against the idea which was only following other newspapers and it took until 4.00pm on the first production day to settle the problem, the management partly winning. But I would not allow the printing of certain sections. As I forecast, the feature did create problems.

Newspaper staff are essential, but so too are newsagents and part-time correspondents. Newsagents throughout my career were the 'eyes' of the industry – they met the buyers face-to-face and knew the likes and dislikes of the readers.

My first newsagent contact was Tim Blackburn, who had his kitchen table as the counter at his terraced house in Wakefield Road, Barnsley. His business was later taken over by Walter Skidmore when he returned from a prisoner of war camp. Walter rented my dad's hen hut in Burton Road to sort his papers, which he then delivered on his motorcycle.

Amos Griffiths and Kay Hellewell in Midland Road, Royston, also picked up newsworthy items from houses they visited. In Cudworth there was Harold Scorah, and in later years, Harry Sutcliffe and Jack Shepherd. These people became my contacts for local news and friends.

Correspondents also had their ears to the ground in the villages and while I was editor I improved the respect they received for their work. Longest-serving was Brenda Waller at Darfield, Margaret Smith of Mapplewell, Stanley Bradford of Denby Dale, Harold Batty of Clayton West and Stan Crossland at Worsbrough Common.

In 1990 a touch of romance came into my office to solve a mystery which I mentioned in my chapter 'Working Years'. The front counter called to ask if anyone had worked with a previous editor called Ronald Yates, because an elderly woman would like to meet them. I had worked for Ronald so went to the counter to find a small poorly-dressed woman who asked: 'Do you know who I am?'

I said I didn't. She then said:

'I am the woman Ronald was to marry 30 years ago and I understand he has died. Did he die of a broken heart?'

I took her to my office and told her I could remember the planned marriage and had made a collection for a present. I gave her a cup of tea and showed her newspaper cuttings reporting his sudden death. Tears came to her eyes.

The staff had always believed the bride-to-be had been jilted by Ronald, so her next comment came as a big surprise. She said:

'It was not Ronald who cancelled the wedding, it was me. When I went home to Ireland to prepare for the day the Roman Catholic priest said I must not marry a non-Catholic and my family agreed with his instruction. I was heartbroken, went to live in London and although now nearly 80-years-old, I have never married. Every day of my life I have been haunted by that decision I made.'

My stuffed ferret given by Reg Mellor is handed to Chronicle *chairman, Sir Nicholas Hewitt, for preservation in the Boardroom.*

She then asked me to take her to the former editor's office where she stood in front of the desk. Again tears came to her eyes as she said: 'That is where I stood when I returned my engagement ring.'
I escorted her to the front door and offered to take her to the railway station for the journey back to London, but she refused. She added: 'I have wanted to do this for years and now I feel I can die happy.' Clutching Ronald's obituary in her hand, she just waved goodbye

My retirement and service to the town was honoured by a civic dinner at the Town Hall, attended by council leaders, officials and second right, front row, my successor, Robert Cockroft.

The day I retired, the Yorkshire Post *gave me a half-page feature with the heading 'Farewell to a news ferret'. They said, 'Distinctly different, Barnsley could not be expected to have a colourless man as editor of its local paper.'*

and walked away down Church Street. The true love story of Ronald Yates and his bride to be.

A weekly newspaper is a community newspaper on which local people and organisations depend, they have no other source on which to draw for news of truly local events, no matter how small. My years as editor had been both stressful and highly satisfying, so when I decided to retire on my sixty-third birthday in 1994, I felt the staff had worked hard and successfully to establish the *Chronicle* as Yorkshire's finest weekly newspaper.

Retirement was hard to accept after such an active newspaper career and for three years I kept busy organising the *Chronicle's* 'Newspaper in Education' scheme, helping schools in Royston, Penistone, Wombwell, Worsbrough and Dearne to produce their own newspapers. It gave teenagers opportunities to develop their own ideas and three schools won national awards for their newspapers.

Even the scholars at Grange Gate Primary School, Lundwood, called for my help in producing their own paper. These ten-year-olds were outstanding and again, won an award for their work.

Once a journalist, always a journalist and looking back on my time as editor, I formed the opinion it was like being a football manager or vicar. It was impossible to please everyone.

Rare Request

*I*t is rare for a weekly newspaper editor to be invited to write a special article for a national newspaper, but in July 1990 such a request came to my office at the *Chronicle*.

Between the lines

Don Booker

Barnsley

Chronicle

● ●

BOB ELLERKER was the best gravedigger in the business. He shaped the grave to the size of the coffin and his finished task in the bowels of the earth was a work of art. Bob had the official title of cemetery curator to Royston Urban Council.

want instant news. Gone are the days of two-column stories — they want short, to-the-point stories and features. That means more stories to be found and written to fill the same space. Direct input may have brought extra cash benefits, but the journalists certainly earn their money.

Even before new technology, the telephone became essential for many aspects of newsgathering, but detrimental in others. In emergencies, stories can be filed in minutes through a contact at the end of the wire, but some lazy or hard-pressed reporters now sit at a desk all day and gather facts by

The Guardian *article in July 1990.*

The *Guardian* had become famous for its Monday media section, and the editor telephoned with a request that I write the leading article for its 'between the lines' column. 'On what subject?' I asked. 'We will leave that to you,' came the reply.

For days I felt rather worried about the request and considered forgetting the idea. Then I thought about the lowering of journalistic standards in news gathering, so I wrote the following article:

'Bob Ellerker was the best gravedigger in the business. He shaped the grave to the size of the coffin and his finished task in the bowels of the earth was a work of art. Bob had the official title of Cemetery Curator to Royston Urban Council. He was even more important than the job title – he was a good news contact, an essential for all weekly newspapers. Michael Parkinson – for the opposition South Yorkshire Times *– and I, started our first days as junior reporters covering the same beat and at 9.00am each weekday morning, we called to see Bob, who lived in a terraced house outside the cemetery gates. More often than not, Bob was deep down, digging a grave and we would shout down: "Have you anything today?"*

Not only would he give names and addresses of those who had died in the past twenty-four hours in the pit village, but also offer items of news he had gathered to help fill our pages. A good graveside manner was essential for young reporters.

Such contacts were essential. Once these folk are confident about the newshounds who call weekly, they will look for titbits of news every day of the week.

Then the weekly newspaper does not have only one reporter in a district, but can finish with sixty. Grassroots reporting is the backbone of a weekly and it is from such news items that national newspapers generate much of their material.

New technology may have improved the profitability of newspapers, but not the quality. It has also meant more time facing a screen for weekly writers, who may produce forty district news paragraphs daily, eight news stories, plus a feature – and all the content having to be found and researched.

Reporters and sub-editors work much harder today than they did ten years ago.

There were times when reporters could fill their papers in two days because pages were few. In recent years they have been faced with bumper issues, including advertising features, bigger news features and supplements.

Just like daily tabloid readers, weekly readers want instant news. Gone are the days of two-column stories – they want short, to-the-point stories and features. That means more stories to be found and written to fill the same space. Direct input may have brought extra cash benefits, but the journalists certainly earn their money.

Even before new technology, the telephone became essential for many aspects of news gathering, but detrimental in others. In emergencies, stories can be filed in minutes through a contact at the end of the wire, but some lazy, hard-pressed reporters now sit at a desk all day and gather facts by telephone.

They miss out on the most fascinating part of being a reporter – meeting people face to face. To know a face means more confidence for a contact. Some newspapers depend heavily on cuttings from other papers. At the Barnsley Chronicle, we stand or fall by our contact system.

Weekly newspapers are the lifeblood of newspaper journalism, not only providing trained staff, but material for their pages. Staff writers and freelancers cannot wait to get their copies of the Chronicle and use its material in the week ahead.

One Sun reporter had the cheek to complain to the general manager when his Friday Chronicle came a day late and missed his Saturday edition. When national papers use our stories, I expose them the following week, complete with their mastheads. It lets our readers know they saw it first in the Chronicle.

Campaigns are good for weekly newspapers and roads, green belt matters and the environment are always good topics.

Being a local paper does not mean one must be dull. The

Chronicle *published a topless model on its front page – taken from the rear, of course – which brought 100 letters of protest. They were all published.*

We also sent Britain's first man into space. Sam Barn, our cartoon character, was taken in the Russian spaceship Mir by Cosmonaut Alexander Volkov, who accepted Sam on a visit to the Chronicle. *On Christmas Day, Sam was beamed to earth through the Noel Edmonds'Television show and sent greetings to the people of Barnsley and the world.*

Such publicity is the PR's dream, but it shows what a weekly can achieve with team work.'

The *Guardian* was delighted with the down-to-earth feature and I received letters and telephone calls from Germany, Ireland and many parts of the UK. They were journalists who agreed with my comments.

Head of Journalism Studies at Stradbroke College, Sheffield, Ron Eyley, sent a letter with the following comment:

'I have just smiled my way through your delightful piece in the Guardian. *Apart from being a lovely piece of writing, it revived wonderful memories of the days when I used to call on the local undertakers as a preliminary to doing daily obituary calls.'*

He decided to include the article in a portfolio about the local reporter's work, for distribution to pre-entry students. Ron also commented:

'Some young people are still joining us who feel that the job is all about putting the world to rights via hard-hitting leaders in the nationals – and nothing else. I don't imagine that they will ever have the fun we had on the local weeklies in the good old days!'

True words from a top journalist.

Through the Lens

Press photographers are a special breed. They always claim to be overworked and sometimes looking at their weekly newspaper diary the claim is obviously true. One wonders how they manage to cover all the events.

The first *Chronicle* photographer was Arthur Littlewood, who also had to make the zinc plates of his photographs for the printing process. He worked in the process engraving department with Fred Farrow, who married Shirley, the clerk I replaced in the advertising department.

In the early days cameramen had to get to jobs by walking or going on the bus. Photographs were taken with a use-and-discard flash bulb, but when these bulbs were first replaced by electronic flash units, they had to struggle to carry all their equipment, which was contained in two large cases. Early cameras also had glass slides, later replaced by strip film. When slides were used, the photographer had to remember to remove the slide before opening the shutter. On one occasion preparing a feature on the activities of Royston teenagers, Geoff Richards took more than eighty photographs, but on developing the plates found they were all clear because he had not removed the slide. He became known as the chap who had made a greenhouse in a day.

As years went on and I became chief reporter and news editor, it was often a problem getting photographers to do what the news room wanted. One photographer always said he was not available between 11.00am and 11.30am. He would be seen leaving the office with the big leather camera case on his shoulder and it was a long time before we discovered he was shopping for his wife – collecting bread from Goodworths, in Market Hill.

Stan Bulmer joined the staff and became a town personality and a regular pressman at Barnsley FC matches at home and away. The crowds would often shout 'Give us a wave, Stan.' Before he arrived we often struggled to get good match cover. On one occasion, forgetting to go to Oakwell, Geoff Richards said he would get a photograph and asked who the visiting team had been. He was told it was Grimsby Town, so Don Oakes looked back in the file and found an old photograph taken during the seasiders' visit the previous season and in which none of the players' faces could be seen clearly.

There was also a problem getting photographs to show a ball in the net. The problem was overcome by superimposing a ball on the photograph. There were at times, other problems where hurriedly taken shots were developed revealing birds and telegraph poles on the heads of people. Company transport for photographers was provided, ranging from a scooter to vans and, eventually, cars. Reg Bagnall, who worked for the *South Yorkshire Times* covered jobs in a Reliant Robin three-wheeler.

There was much repetition on a weekly newspaper diary and photographers would often moan about covering the same type of job, even when the previous occasion had been a year earlier.

Wes Hobson had worked in the paper's studio and when a rare vacancy occurred in the photographic department he applied and was appointed. What a wonderful photographer he proved to be, showing much flair, but not having a lot of luck. Visiting Gawber Primary School to photograph a pet goat, he decided to get the pet in the frame of its shed door. He got inside when suddenly there was a thunderstorm and the goat bolted back into the shed, the door closing behind it. Wes was rescued from his temporary prison by a girl who had been on the playing field and saw what happened.

While taking holiday photographs at Barnsley Metrodome swimming pool, he set up a youngster near the waterfall. Stepping back to get the right angle, he duly fell in the pool. Travelling to a job, he became trapped between the barriers at the Jumble Lane railway crossing when a bus in front continually allowed other vehicles to go first, with him stuck on the line as the barrier came down. Wes had to dash to the signal-box and ask for the barrier to be lifted!

Setting up a photograph with Lord Mason of Barnsley on the field at Oakwell, Wes called him Lord Nelson, only realising what he had said when a security man reminded him. Don Oakes was popular with local organisations and schools where he had been taking photographs of their annual events for over twenty years. He was so popular with one group that the lady secretary made him an unusual request: 'I'm a good artist and I would love to paint a nude picture of you.' We never found out if the request had been granted. Another photographer, Roy Sabine, covering a play at Penistone Drill Hall, had problems getting all the cast in the frame. He stepped back, fell off the stage and as the cast gasped, he clicked his shutter and got a rare shot, while on his back on the floor.

Great strides have been made in photographic production. During my time as editor it would take four days to process a colour photograph. Now it can be less than ten minutes.

Naked Truth

A 30-year mystery was only solved at the retirement lunch I gave for my editorial staff at Silkstone Golf Club.

The staff presented me with a wall clock bought at a car boot sale and a photograph of a nude woman posing on my desk in the 1970s... and it solved my mystery. In my early days of motoring writing I was often baffled by white powder on my desk each morning, powder that often covered my sleeves and elbows.

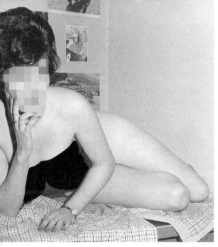

photograph presented to me by Keith Lodge [a]ny retirement dinner which solved the 'white [pow]der' mystery.

Although I asked questions, I never found the answer until the day I retired. The staff now explained.

I had a nice, secluded office and the photographers had noted this convenient facility. After visiting nightclubs where they picked up local lasses, they went back with them to my office to take nude photographs.

The photographer, in truly gentlemanly fashion, would place his raincoat on my desk and the young lady would pose. Perfume was very expensive at the time and the girls used talcum powder as a deodorant and perfume.

My staff knew I had long been puzzled about the white powder, so they had the photograph framed, thus solving the mystery on my last day at the *Chronicle*.

The staff sprang the surprise and it brought a humorous end to my days with the newspaper.

One of the photographs was given by chief photographer Geoff Richards, to a colleague's father in hospital who had had a heart attack, to aid his recovery. It did the trick. When he died twenty years later the photograph was found among his belongings.

Honours

H onours rarely come the way of journalists. The first I received being from Chief Scout, William Gladstone, who in 1974 awarded me the Medal of Merit, in recognition of my services to the Movement.

On 14 November 1994, a letter arrived from the Prime Minister's Office. It was from his Principal Private Secretary and read:

> *'The Prime Minister has asked me to inform you, in strict confidence, that he has it in mind, on the occasion of the forthcoming list of New Year Honours, to submit your name to The Queen with a recommendation that Her Majesty may be graciously pleased to approve that you be appointed a Member of the Order of the British Empire.'*

It was for 'Services to journalism and the community of Barnsley' and came seven months after my retirement. I felt it a great honour

both for me and for journalism and I appreciated that it would not have happened without the wonderful support I had had both from colleagues and members of organisations with which I had been associated.

The family's great day was Valentine's Day, Tuesday, 14 February 1995, when Freda, Julie, Lucy and Simon went to Buckingham Palace for the investiture. It is difficult to

Above: At Sheffield's Cutlers Hall, Sir Eric Mensforth presented me with Scouting's Medal of Merit, watched by the Master Cutler and County Secretary, Percy Twine.

Guild of Motoring Writers' President Lord Strathcarron presents my first writing award, the Motorcycle Writer of the Year Award at London's RAC Club in 1979.

Her Majesty the Queen chats after presenting the MBE in the State Room.

On those famous steps outside the Palace.

Lucy holds the MBE as the family celebrate a memorable Valentine's Day.

describe the emotions we felt in the Palace courtyard and as we passed along the corridors lined with colourful guardsmen and the mounting excitement when we heard the orchestra playing in the State Room.

As with other recipients, a small clip was placed on my lapel on which the Queen would hang the medal and in the picture gallery our names were checked ten times as we were briefed on procedure. There was diligent attention to detail.

Seeing the Yeoman of the Guard and the famous Gurkhas escorting the Queen, one reflected only England could offer such pageantry. It made one look back on one's life.

I should have bowed twice, but managed three times. In those few moments of privacy with the Queen, her gentle handshake, thoughtful comments and her smile made me realise what a wonderful nation we have and should appreciate.

She spoke about the *Chronicle* and thought it was a miracle how papers were produced so quickly. She also wished every success to St Peter's Hospice.

There were no refreshments after the ceremony, as many people think, but the 120 recipients just chatted about the most wonderful day in their lives. That pathway to honour is usually only trodden once in a lifetime.

As a family we then went to St Paul's Cathedral to the Order of the British Empire Chapel which is in the crypt. Because I was a member of the Order, Julie could have been married there and Lucy baptised in the crypt.

In those moments of silence, I felt it would have been wonderful if my parents had been able to share the honour and joy of the occasion.

It was a day we will never forget, but the honour for me was tinged with sadness. Every organisation with which I had been associated and most other aspects of my life had a Christian basis or connection, yet in my own church the honour was never mentioned. It was felt to be a secular honour.

My fellow churchwarden, Pat Micklethwaite made a secret collection to present a gift to mark the Queen's award, but even the presentation did not take place in church. People were ushered into the nearby community centre.

Among the many congratulatory messages was one which gave me particular pleasure. It was from the Newspaper Society. It said that during 1995, I was the only newspaper editor to be so honoured.

On the first day of the new millennium I was included in

Presentation of Barnsley's Millennium Medal by the Mayor and Lord Lieutenant.

Barnsley's first Millennium Awards of Merit List. It meant I had been honoured by the Queen and my home town within five years of retiring from the *Chronicle*.

Over 100 nominations were made of people whom, residents of the town thought had made a contribution to the well-being of Barnsley. Only twenty were chosen and I received a special sterling silver medal and scroll from the Mayor, Cllr Howard Lavender and the Lord Lieutenant of South Yorkshire, the Earl of Scarbrough, at a civic reception in the Town Hall.

It was given for service to the hospice movement, and nearly 60 years to Scouting, and St Paul's Church.

One never expects to be honoured by the Queen and then local people, but as I said in my opening comments, without other people around us we would be nothing in life and achieve little.

A further contact with royalty came on 7 August 2000, when Audi UK invited me to dinner on the Royal Yacht Britannia at Leith, Edinburgh. In the State dining room I was asked to give the after-dinner vote of thanks to mark the launch of their A2 car.

Epilogue

A fter reading about my colourful and hectic life, you may want to rest awhile.

I could not have had a more wonderful life, even if I had left my much-loved Barnsley. Some of my experiences and views may do some good and make some people think. A few secrets have been revealed. The people of Barnsley have taught me the best things in life. These include being forthright and honest and to care about others along a road that at times has been very difficult. A good family and friends are the foundation of life and in this direction I have been fortunate. My profession is the most exciting in the world. However, I am not sure that I would be attracted to a career in journalism in the new millennium with its near total dependence on desk-bound technology and lack of face-to-face communication with people due to the continual use of the telephone. They are wonderful tools of the trade, but eliminate the thrill of meeting people which this book proves is such a fascinating part of life.

Good news-gathering is labour intensive and costly. That is why new technology is so successful for managements, but has not improved newspaper content. Like my friend Michael Parkinson, I have never mastered computers, but they do not make writers. Michael had his first word about our chin-strap trilby crash hats. I will have the last - I don't think he did use his Aunt Madge's knicker elastic. As junior reporters, we had a fulfilling and eventful start in grass-roots journalism. The preceding chapters prove what can be achieved and how life is so full of interest. Also that one of the finest things in life is to have a good laugh and share it with others.

If this book has at times put a smile on your face, then it has achieved its objective. Thanks to you all.

Acknowledgements
Herbert Taylor, Doris Brown, Phillip Brown, Des Horsley, Ron Harris, Brian Panks, Gordon Broadbent, Harold Fearn, Keith Ward, Audrey Moxon, William Chatterton, Frank Chatterton, Ernest Horbury, *Barnsley Chronicle*, Barnsley Archives.

Photograph Acknowledgements
Old Barnsley Book Shop - front cover, Cris Haigh Photography - back cover, *Barnsley Chronicle*, John Marshall, Bonham-Carter Associates Ltd, Charles Green, Thames Television.